THE KENNEDY ASSASSINATION

THE TRUTH BEHIND THE CONSPIRACY THAT KILLED THE PRESIDENT

DAVID SOUTHWELL

CARLTON
BOOKS

Contents

Introduction

There are collisions of time and space which form nexus points in history. A moment of decision or a brutal instant of death that will shatter the present and forever determine the path of events which follow. Dallas, 12:30 pm Central Standard Time on Friday, November 22, 1963 is one of those nexus points.

Whatever else you believe about the death of John F. Kennedy on that momentous day, it takes an act of overwhelming denial not to recognize its impact upon history. Not just a husband and father died. Not just an American President. A world-shaper died. As the Cuban Missile Crisis had proved, the decisions of JFK could and did decide the fate of the world.

I was nine years old when I first read about JFK's assassination in a *Bumper Book of Mysteries*. I was thrilled to discover what I thought was the biggest unsolved murder mystery ever. I already knew adults lied about important things, so it came as no shock to discover the covered-up evidence which suggested Lee Harvey Oswald did not act alone.

It was exciting to discover about witnesses who thought the shots came from the grassy knoll. The fact that top marksmen could not replicate the three shots fired in the time Lee was meant to have taken. The astonishing information that the one bit of proof which could clear up whether it was a conspiracy or not—the President's brain—was missing.

I have been fascinated ever since reading that first book. I am not alone in my fascination. There have been effectively three governmental reports and more than 1,000 books on JFK's death published, all seeking to answer the question of who killed Kennedy? For a huge swathe of people, the question remains unanswered to their satisfaction.

Today, there are tens of thousands of websites which support a conspiracy and which ask over and over, three basic questions: Who had the motive? Who had the ability to actually pull off a successful assassination of the President? Who had the power to cover up such a conspiracy and ensure that no-one involved ever came to justice?

There are thousands of facts relating to the case which can be taken from the overwhelming number of official documents. Witness statements to FBI memos, forensic evidence and autopsy photos to painstaking analysis of films and photographs, you can easily assemble a collection of facts which backs up the theory that Lee Harvey Oswald was not a lone gunman. However, from the same assortment of evidence, one can make a case suggesting the exact reverse.

Across the years I have upset a lot of conspiracy theorists by saying that 95 percent of all conspiracy theories are rubbish. I stand by that statement. Yet the 5 percent that are not nonsense are incredibly important. Having spent years researching the assassination of JFK, I firmly believe it may be the most provable and significant conspiracy in living memory.

However, being able to prove that there was a conspiracy rarely tells us anything in terms of actual fact as to who carried it out and why. This is certainly true in the murder of JFK. Even if a researcher could prove who actually killed Kennedy, it would be beyond arrogant for anyone to claim to have solved all of the strange elements that make up the wider conspiracy. There are simply too many mysteries spiralling back to that nexus point in Dealey Plaza.

Two decades ago, I spoke to the great American comedian and conspiracy theorist adherent Bill Hicks. We talked about Waco conspiracy theories, about NASA conspiracies, and we talked about JFK. To him, it was "the ground zero of conspiracy culture."

Beyond his anger at what he saw as a coup d'état, a stealing of the Government from its people by an elite, Bill was angry that people asked him why he got so worked up about the assassination. His voice rose beyond the mock anger of a comedy routine into a frighteningly forceful rant.

"I get so sick of the debunkers. Even more than that, I get so sick of those idiots asking me 'why it still matters?' They killed a man. They stole your Government. They stole the history we should have had. That's why it matters. Do you think we would have been here today, like this, with another four years of JFK? Eight years of Bobby after that? However many years on, that's why it matters. Those shots still echo."

Suddenly his voice fell back to a soft Texan crawl. "It matters. Those shots still echo."

Bill Hicks was definitely right on one thing. We all live in the temporal shadow of Dallas. Those shots still do echo and whilst they do, it is right to keep asking the fundamental question: Who killed Kennedy?

OPPOSITE, TOP A new hope. As a Democratic presidential candidate in 1960, Senator John F. Kennedy manifests the hopes and dreams of many Americans wanting to move from fear into an era of peace and progress.

OPPOSITE, BOTTOM Into the crosshairs of history—President John F. Kennedy and First Lady Jacqueline Kennedy ride triumphantly through the crowded streets of Dallas, unaware they are traveling inextricably toward the shadow of death.

RIGHT On top of the world. JFK and Jackie enjoy a ride up Broadway during a ticker-tape parade. The myth of the Kennedys' Camelot has entered the collective unconscious, but dark forces haunted his presidency right from the start of the campaign trail.

Kennedy's Early Career and the Kennedy Clan

The assassination of John Fitzgerald Kennedy on November 22, 1963, has such powerful gravity in our imaginations that it tends to warp our assessment of him as both man and politician. Yet the bare facts alone make Kennedy remarkable. As the 35th president of the United States, he was the youngest elected to that office and its only Catholic president. A Pulitzer Prize-winner and war hero, he became the image of the new America that was emerging in the early 1960s.

 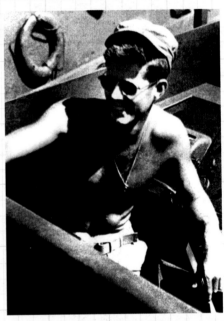

ABOVE LEFT Groomed for success. Joseph Kennedy Sr. with his sons John and Joseph Jr. (Joe) in London, 1937, when Joseph Sr. was stationed there as American ambassador. Once it became clear he would not achieve the presidency himself, he transferred his hopes to his sons.

ABOVE RIGHT Action man—naval lieutenant, decorated war hero, and future President John F. Kennedy on board the torpedo boat he commanded in the Southwest Pacific during World War II.

From the moment of his birth on May 29, 1917, John F. Kennedy could not be said to be an average American. He was born into a prominent family that enjoyed a position of wealth and high-level influence within Boston's Irish community. JFK's father, Joseph P. Kennedy, was a businessman and political insider who managed to cultivate influence and carve a fortune worth more than $2.8 billion in today's terms.

Despite legitimate investments in banking, movie production, and real estate, Joseph P. Kennedy was never able to escape the popular belief that his fortune came from bootlegging alcohol during Prohibition. He certainly had contact with gangsters such as Frank Costello—known as the "prime minister of the underworld"—and head of the Chicago Syndicate Sam "Momo" Giancana. Joseph even invested money in a Florida racetrack with key Mafia associate Meyer Lansky.

Joseph P. Kennedy's role in funding Franklin Roosevelt's successful bid for the presidency in 1932 was rewarded with his appointment as ambassador to the Court of St. James (United Kingdom) in 1938. Both JFK and his elder brother Joseph Jr. studied at the London School of Economics whilst their father became an increasingly controversial figure. Joseph proposed appeasing Hitler and opposed giving Britain military and economic aid. Former British Cabinet member Josiah Wedgwood described the ambassador as "a rich man, untrained in diplomacy, unlearned in history, a great publicity seeker and who apparently is ambitious to be the first Catholic president of the U.S."

However, Joseph's falling out with President Roosevelt over foreign policy and remarks such as "Democracy is finished in England. It may be here too," helped end his presidential ambitions. Instead he concentrated on getting his sons elected to the highest office. When Joseph Jr. was killed on a bombing run in 1944, his father put all of his dynastic desire behind JFK and his younger brother Robert F. Kennedy.

John F. Kennedy was disqualified from the U.S. Army in 1941 owing to back problems. Using contacts with the Office of Naval Intelligence, he managed to get himself assigned to the navy, rising to the rank of lieutenant and commanding a torpedo patrol boat. When his boat was rammed by the Japanese destroyer *Amagiri*, JFK towed a badly injured crewman to safety on an island with a life-jacket strap held between his teeth. For this act of bravery, he was awarded the Navy and Marine Corps Medal.

In 1947, being a decorated war hero and his father's political muscle helped John F. Kennedy to become the U.S. representative for the 11th congressional district in Massachusetts. By 1952, he was well enough established as a politician to take on the incumbent Republican Henry Cabot Lodge, Jr. and become a U.S. Senator from Massachusetts. During

his first year as a Senator, JFK married businessman's daughter Jacqueline Lee Bouvier.

Over the next two years, JFK underwent many operations for chronic back pain. At one point he was so ill that the last rites were administered. His health problems were so severe that he was often absent from the Senate. However, during convalescence, he managed to publish a book entitled *Profiles In Courage* (covering a selection of Senators) which won him a Pulitzer Prize for biography. Later, claims would be made that Kennedy's speechwriter Ted Sorensen had ghostwritten the book for him.

John F. Kennedy failed in the ballot to become the Democrat candidate for Vice President in 1956. This was in part the result of the poor view many liberals in his party had of his family's close association with the discredited anti-communist Senator Joseph McCarthy. When JFK entered into the race to become the Democrats' candidate for President in 1960, therefore, it was as an underdog.

In the primaries for his party's nomination, his father's money allowed for unprecedented levels of campaign advertising, but it was JFK's personal charm and public tackling of anti-Catholic prejudice that did more to achieve notable victories in Wisconsin and West Virginia. By the time he had secured the nomination for President, a carefully crafted image of Kennedy as a vigorous young leader, skilled politician, and highly moral and loving family man had been developed. It was an image accepted by a significant proportion of Americans, and one that helped propel him toward fulfilling Joseph Kennedy's dream of seeing his son in the White House.

However, the shadowed truth about JFK was somewhat different.

ABOVE Crowd pleaser. Senator John F. Kennedy works an enthusiastic crowd with his wife Jackie while campaigning for President in the 1960 election.

BELOW Christmas at Camelot. President John F. Kennedy and First Lady Jacqueline Kennedy pose with their family and Jackie's sister and brother-in-law on Christmas Day at the White House, Washington, D.C., December 25, 1962. From left: Caroline Kennedy, unidentified, John F. Kennedy Jr., Jackie Kennedy, Anthony Radziwill, JFK, Prince Stanislaus Radziwill, Lee Radziwill, and Ann Christine Radziwill.

JACQUELINE KENNEDY

During JFK's presidency, Jacqueline Kennedy was transformed in the eyes of most of America from a somewhat effete electoral liability—her elite background was evidenced by her fluency in French—into a fashion icon and emblematic ideal of a political wife. Spending $45,446 of her husband's first-year $100,000 presidential salary on fashion by designers such as Oleg Cassini, Dior, Givenchy, and Chanel gave rise to the "Jackie" look that still enjoys periodic revivals. Her management of the White House restoration turned it into an iconic showcase of American history, art, and literature. As First Lady; she was the epitome of motherhood and style, and she helped to bring glamor and celebrity to politics. However, the public image was heavily manipulated, and her use of the amphetamine Dexedrine and her pain at JFK's affairs were kept well away from public scrutiny.

Kennedy's Controversies

Modern opinion polls among the American public regularly rank JFK as one of the greatest presidents of all time. Yet contemporary views of his presidency were more muted. Before the tragedy of his murder clouded memory and judgement, approval of Kennedy as either President or a man was often hard to find. The 1,036-day span of his presidency was not free from considerable controversy.

ABOVE Castro's Cuban forces use heavy artillery to pound the American-backed rebels during the unsuccessful Operation Zapata. The failed invasion became known as the Bay of Pigs disaster and cast a long, sinister shadow across JFK's presidency.

BELOW A dirty business. Senator John F. Kennedy and Vice-President Richard Nixon during the intense second televised presidential debate. Kennedy's slim victory in the 1960 election was partly the result of alleged electoral fraud.

Most newly elected presidents are gifted with at least a short honeymoon period. However, the nature of Kennedy's election victory robbed him of any hope of that. Even more than the disputed 2000 presidential election between George W. Bush and Al Gore, Kennedy's win has been recorded in history as a stolen election.

The 1960 campaign for the White House between John F. Kennedy and Richard Nixon had been one of the bitterest ever seen. When the votes were tallied, JFK achieved victory by an incredibly slim margin. The result rested on just two states—Texas and Illinois. However it was clear there had been widespread fraud across Texas and especially in Cook County, Illinois.

In one Texas county there were only 4,895 registered voters, but 6,138 votes cast—with more than 75 percent favoring Kennedy. In Chicago, voters occupying cemetery plots voted for Kennedy and when one reporter went to an address where 56 Kennedy voters were registered, he found the building long demolished. A Department of Justice investigation into election fraud aroused suspicions of a cover-up as the head of the DOJ was none other than U.S. Attorney-General Robert F. Kennedy.

Nixon was urged by his aides to challenge the result. He refused, saying: "It would tear the country to pieces. You can't do that." However, Nixon nursed a harsh grudge, repeatedly telling close colleagues: "That son of a bitch Kennedy stole it."

The electoral fraud was not the only grudge Nixon held against Kennedy. During the election, JFK received a top-secret briefing on a proposed invasion of Cuba by a CIA-trained force of Cuban exiles in an attempt to overthrow Fidel Castro. In their fourth TV debate, Kennedy broke this

trust and called on Nixon to support just such an idea. For reasons of national security, Nixon had to be seen to deny such a plan, attacking it as "dangerously irresponsible." This made him look weak on Cuba.

On the advice of CIA director Allen Dulles and his senior generals, Kennedy continued to back the secret invasion plans when he became President. On January 21, 1961, Kennedy authorized Operation Zapata—a CIA-backed invasion of the Bay of Pigs some 90 miles south-east of the capital Havana. However, the CIA lied to JFK, failing to tell him Soviet radio stations were predicting "a CIA-hatched plot using paid criminals" a week before it was set to be launched.

The resulting Bay of Pigs invasion was a complete disaster. Within three days of the invasion starting, 114 Cuban exiles from what was known as Brigade 2506 were dead as were four American airmen. Hundreds of Cuban exiles and several CIA operatives were later executed by Castro's forces, who also held prisoner more than 1,200 invaders.

The extreme embarrassment to the Kennedy Administration caused by the Bay of Pigs made it reluctant to back any further military intervention in Cuba. This resulted in virulent anti-Kennedy feeling among many Cuban exiles and CIA agents involved in the invasion such as E. Howard Hunt. Kennedy subsequently sacked Dulles and was so enraged with the failure of the CIA that he declared he would splinter it into "a thousand pieces and scatter it to the winds." Kennedy also told journalist Ben Bradlee: "The first advice I'm giving my successor is watch the generals."

On the domestic front, the Kennedy Administration was mired down when it came to making progress on the key issue of ending state-sanctioned racial discrimination. During his presidency, the issue of civil rights spiraled from turbulence to increasing violence and murder. JFK found himself in the firing line of both sides.

To the right-wingers and many white southern Democrats, Kennedy was dangerously eroding the power of the states. To the black community, he

ABOVE More than 200,000 protesters gather to demand equal rights for black Americans on Constitution Avenue in Washington, D.C. during August 1963. Among them is key civil rights campaigner Martin Luther King Jr. (fourth from left).

BELOW Mariella Novotny was a prostitute who worked out of the infamous Quorum Club in Washington, DC. As well as enjoying an affair with JFK, she was embroiled in the Profumo sex scandal in London in 1963.

was betraying the support that he had promised for racial integration and civil rights during the 1960 election. Despite his pro-civil rights speeches in 1963, JFK seemed powerless to stop a rising tide of blood against those who wanted an end to the persecution of black Americans.

Even an event now judged to be one of Kennedy's finest displays of statesmanship—the successful avoiding of a nuclear war during the Cuban Missile Crisis—was seen by many Americans at the time as capitulation to communism. General Curtis LeMay told the President: "It is the greatest defeat in our history." It was a view shared by many in the military, the CIA, and America's right-wing.

ALL THE PRESIDENT'S WOMEN

JFK enjoyed a public image as a doting father and devoted husband, an image carefully constructed from a stream of relaxed family snapshots and home movies. However, behind the media surface was a different, dissonant reality. Kennedy enjoyed a string of affairs with women throughout his marriage. Most of them were known about and tolerated by his wife. The women ranged from White House staff such as Marion "Mimi" Beardsley and Jill S. Cowan to women with more dubious reputations, including Mariella Novotny—an English prostitute linked to the Profumo Affair. Worryingly, Kennedy shared a bed with possible East German spy Ellen Rometsch and with Judith Exner, the mistress of Mafia boss Sam Giancana. However, there is no evidence to substantiate rumors that JFK slept with Marilyn Monroe.

Prelude to a Killing

Every choice has invisible antecedents. The fall of dominos leading to JFK's assassination may have begun on June 5, 1963, when Kennedy met with his Texan Vice President Lyndon B. Johnson and Texas Governor John Connally in El Paso, Texas. A fund-raising and support-boosting trip to Texas was agreed on ahead of the 1964 presidential election. Kennedy had barely won Texas in 1960 and hoped the visit would help him in the state. He also hoped to end the conflict between his ally Senator Ralph Yarborough and LBJ supporter Governor Connally.

K ennedy may not have known he was heading to his death by agreeing to the trip, but others seemed to. On November 20, Rose Cheramie—a former stripper for Jack Ruby (the nightclub owner later convicted of the murder of Lee Harvey Oswald)—was hit by a car on Highway 190 in Louisiana. She was taken to a private hospital, but as she was exhibiting signs of drug withdrawal, Lt. Francis Frugé of the Louisiana State Police was called. While Frugé was transporting Rose to another hospital, she told him she had been traveling to Galveston, Texas as a drug courier for Jack Ruby and that the two men she was traveling with were going to kill the President in Dallas in a few days. She repeated the claims to a hospital psychiatrist and nurses.

Frugé originally thought her story was drug-withdrawal ramblings, but after the assassination he interviewed Rose. Finding the details of what she said to be factually accurate, Frugé's boss rang Captain Will Fritz of the Dallas Police. Fritz was not interested. Rose Cheramie died in Texas in 1965 after being hit by a car on Highway 155.

Eugene Dinkin was a U.S. army cryptographic operator based in Metz, France. On November 4, 1963, Dinkin went AWOL. Two days later he appeared in the press room of the UN in Geneva, telling reporters of a plot against Kennedy and that "something would happen in Dallas." On November 13, Dinkin was arrested and placed in a military psychiatric hospital. A comrade reported that he had told him the assassination would happen on November 22. Although the Warren Commission was aware of Dinkin's allegations, they did not investigate. CIA documents on Dinkin submitted to them were classified and not available to the public, as were calls made to the U.S. Naval Attaché in Australia, Lt. Commander Piper, warning him of a plot to kill Kennedy ahead of the assassination.

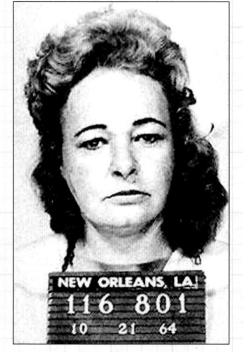

LEFT Prophetess of doom. The police mug shot of Rose Cheramie, former stripper and self-confessed drug runner for Jack Ruby. Cheramie was one of a handful of people who appear to have had genuine and provable foreknowledge of the fact that President Kennedy was to be assassinated in Dallas.

BELOW Lord of lies. The man known as "Tricky Dicky" was infamous for having a strained relationship with the truth, even for a politician. However, why did he lie about where he was when he first heard of Kennedy's death?

WHAT WAS NIXON DOING IN DALLAS?

As with 9/11 for a later generation, those Americans alive at the time can all remember where they were when they heard that JFK had been killed. Everyone except Richard Nixon. He used to tell a strange white lie and say he was in a New York cab flagged down by a crying woman when he discovered the news. He wasn't. Newspaper reports prove that he knew about the death when he got off a plane in New York that had just flown in from Dallas. He had been in the city between November 20 and 22, holding meetings. He may even have heard of JFK's death while attending a Pepsi-Cola conference in Dallas on November 22. Whether or not he was at the infamous Murchison meeting (see page 11,) Nixon was with actress and Pepsi heiress Joan Crawford on November 21 in Dallas when she made oddly prophetic comments about them not needing security to visit the city, unlike JFK.

LEFT The last hours. Flanked by (left to right) Senator Ralph Yarborough, Texas Governor John Connally, and Vice President Lyndon Johnson, President Kennedy addresses the crowds gathered to see him at Forth Worth, Texas on the morning of November 22.

BELOW Dallas, nut country. When JFK saw the virulent attack on him in a full-page ad in the *Dallas Morning News* entitled "Welcome Mr. Kennedy To Dallas" paid for by members of the Hunt oil dynasty, he referred to Dallas as "nut country." Therefore the size and warmth of the crowds greeting him in the city came as a huge surprise.

Another individual with near-prophetic abilities was right-wing extremist Joseph Milteer. On November 10, 1963, Miami police provided a tape to the FBI and the Secret Service made by an informant who had infiltrated a far-right group. On it was a recording of Milteer saying that there was a plot to kill JFK "From an office building with a high-powered rifle... They will pick somebody up within hours afterwards... Just to throw the public off." Despite this, the FBI and Secret Service did not interview Milteer, nor did they strengthen security for the President in Dallas.

The decision of the Secret Service not to improve protection in Dallas seems even stranger given that American U.N. ambassador Adlai Stevenson was heckled, spat on, and physically attacked by right-wing activists while in Dallas on October 24. Stevenson feared Kennedy would face similar antagonism and warned him not to go to Dallas. After the attack on Stevenson, Dallas was officially declared a hostile city, but instead of following established protocols for such an environment, the Secret Service actually reduced security by taking off the limousine's bubble-top, not riding on the back of the car, and allowing open windows along the route. The 112th Military Intelligence Group at Fort Sam in Texas was ordered to stand down on presidential security despite the protests of the unit's commander Colonel Reich.

Lyndon B. Johnson's mistress Madeleine Brown later alleged that on November 20 or 21, a meeting was held at the home of Texas oilman Clint Murchison. Supposedly among those in attendance were LBJ, Richard Nixon, oilman H.L. Hunt, and banker and later Warren Commission member John McCloy. According to Brown, after the meeting LBJ emerged and told her: "That son-of-bastard Yarborough and that god damn f***ing Irish mafia bastard Kennedy will never embarrass me again."

Whatever had caused LBJ to make such a statement, he was to give no indication of it as he, Connally, and Yarborough watched the President address a rally in Fort Worth on the morning of November 22. Despite rain, a crowd of several thousand responded positively to JFK's message of space exploration, American prosperity, and American strength. Once his words ended, Kennedy reached out into a friendly mass of outstretched arms, shaking hands and exchanging smiles. As he drove to Carswell Air Force Base for the 13-minute flight to Dallas, he had no idea how words from his last speech—"This is a very dangerous and uncertain world"—were about to sound chillingly prescient.

Lee Harvey Oswald

Nothing about Lee Harvey Oswald makes sense. The more energy you put into examining his life, the more it becomes a fractal explosion of unfolding mysteries. How was a defector who told officials he was going to give the Soviets secrets allowed to return home without punishment? How did an average marksman pull off shots none of the U.S. government's best marksmen could accomplish? Why does evidence show him as being in two places at the same time?

The biggest question is why he would shoot John F. Kennedy. Even the Warren Commission failed to provide a convincing explanation for his motives. They could only offer: "Oswald was moved by an overriding hostility to his environment." If you are trying to suggest that the highest-profile murder in American history is the work of a lone gunman, not making a convincing argument as to his actual motivation for the killing is a huge drawback.

If there was a conspiracy, it was designed to involve Oswald—either as an active player or as a patsy. If there was a conspiracy, it was also designed to be a double murder, with Oswald set to be the second victim. A corpse that could not answer questions, but that of a man whose high-profile Marxist and pro-Castro views would suggest a set of obvious conclusions which would not be challenged at trial. However, across the decades, researchers have unearthed hundreds of questions about Oswald that have never been satisfactorily answered.

Lee Harvey Oswald was born in New Orleans in 1939. As a teenager he was a member of a Civil Air Patrol group run by David Ferrie (see page 34.) In October 1956, aged 17, Lee enlisted in the United States Marine

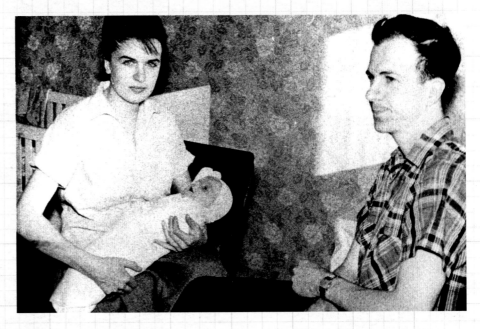

Corps. His career as a radar operator meant a security clearance allowing him to be posted to the CIA's U-2 spy-plane base in Atsugi, Japan. This was despite him openly professing himself a Marxist and pro-Soviet. Unusually, he received training in Russian while in the Marines, though he never qualified as an expert marksman. Among Lee's friends in the Marines was Kerry Thornley. In 1962, Thornley wrote a novel called *The Idle Warriors* about a marine defecting to Russia, based on Oswald.

In October 1959, Oswald traveled to Moscow. Once there, he announced his intention to give radar secrets to the Soviets and handed his passport to the U.S. Embassy. Oswald spent the next 19 months in Russia, marrying Marina Prusakova, the niece of a KGB colonel. Strangely, while Oswald was in Russia, someone in New Orleans used his identity to buy trucks for the pro-Castro

ABOVE Family man. Lee Harvey Oswald, his wife Marina, and their daughter June Lee, taken while the family was living in the Soviet Union. Why was a former Marine who proclaimed in advance he would give military secrets to the Russians allowed to return to the United States without censure?

LEFT Will the Real Lee Harvey Oswald please step forward? Oswald distributes Hands Off Cuba flyers on the streets of New Orleans, Louisiana. However, at the time he did this he was working out of the same offices as anti-Castro campaigners and often seen in the company of anti-Castro Cuban exiles. What were his true sympathies? What was he really up to?

THE ODD COUPLE—
GEORGE DE MOHRENSCHILDT AND OSWALD

Among the multitude of things about Oswald so contradictory that they defy sense is his relationship with George de Mohrenschildt. There is no logic to explain why a Marxist defector would be best friends with a wealthy, rabidly anti-communist Russian émigré and supporter of the National Alliance of Russian Solidarists (N.T.S.)—an anti-Soviet group founded by MI6 and run by the CIA. George de Mohrenschildt was 35 years older than Oswald and an openly right-wing extremist. Involved in the oil business, he counted George H.W. Bush, H.L. Hunt, and Clint Murchison among his friends, and was not a natural companion for Oswald. Why the two were friends remains a striking mystery. In 1977, de Mohrenschildt admitted discussing befriending Oswald with the CIA's Domestic Contact Division, and his later career saw him working with the CIA in Haiti. Many conspiriologists have asked, was he working with them before in looking after Oswald?

ABOVE RIGHT A Very Soviet Union?—The Oswalds in Minsk, 1959. Lee Harvey Oswald met his future wife Marina Marina Prusakova at a trade union dance whilst he was working in a factory in Minsk in 1959. The backgrounds of the couple made them an odd pair for George de Mohrenschildt to befriend.

RIGHT Faked. This infamous photo of Oswald, allegedly found in the home of his friend Ruth Paine, contains more than a dozen elements which lead many photographic experts to conclude it was forged to incriminate Oswald. Among the issues are shadows falling in different directions and no finger tips on the right hand. In questioning, Oswald himself claimed it was an obvious composite.

Friends of Democratic Cuba group linked to Guy Banister, a private investigator and former FBI agent. An FBI memo from 1960 also shows someone in America using Lee's identity.

In May 1962, Oswald, Marina, and their daughter applied to leave the Soviet Union for America. Marina's leaving was not blocked by the Soviets and, despite previously announcing himself a traitor, Oswald was given a repatriation loan and faced no charges. This was without precedent. On his return to Texas, Oswald—although a former traitor—got a job at Jaggar-Chiles-Stoval, a company doing classified map work for the U.S. Army. This was beyond odd. As is the idea that instead of anonymously buying guns from any Texan retailer, Oswald used the alias A.J. Hidell to buy a revolver and rifle by mail order.

Between April and September 1963, Oswald was in New Orleans. He was seen among anti-Castro Cuban exiles working with Guy Banister while at the same time operating a one-man branch of the pro-Castro Fair Play for Cuba Committee. Back in Texas in September, the supposedly Marxist pro-Castro Oswald was introduced to Cuban exile Silvia Odio as "Leon," an American involved in a plan to assassinate Castro.

At the same time that "Leon" was introduced to Odio, Oswald is alleged to have been in Mexico, visiting the Cuban and Soviet embassies. CIA photos claiming to show Oswald doing this are clearly not him. On November 23, the FBI sent a memo to the White House advising that someone impersonating Oswald had phoned and visited the Soviet Embassy in Mexico but that the "individual was not Lee Harvey Oswald."

One clear fact is that in October, three weeks after JFK's Dallas trip was announced, Oswald's friend Ruth Paine helped him get a job at the Texas School Book Depository.

All the odd elements of Oswald's life have led many to claim he must have been working for U.S. intelligence. Some such as John Armstrong even claim there must have been two Oswalds. With his tax returns, Office of Naval Intelligence files, and dozens of CIA files relating to Oswald still classified, it is impossible to know the truth, or to solve the mystery of Lee Harvey Oswald. One thing is certain; the wildest theory about Oswald is that there was anything simple about this alleged lone gunman.

The Assassination

At 11:40am, Air Force One touched down at Love Field in Dallas. The sky was gin-bottle blue and cloud-free, the weather warmer than forecast when Jackie Kennedy had decided to wear a pink Chanel wool suit. As the First Lady stepped from the plane, she was handed a bouquet of blood-red roses. The shouts of an elated crowd roared toward President Kennedy and his wife.

JAMES POWELL AND THE FAKE SECRET SERVICE AGENTS OF DEALEY PLAZA

After the shooting, there were officially no Secret Service agents in Dealey Plaza until Forrest Sorrels, the Secret Service agent in charge of the Dallas office, returned to the area from Parkland Memorial Hospital at 1:00pm. However, testimony from witnesses reveals several men flashed credentials and claimed to be Secret Service in the aftermath of the murder. Conspiracy debunkers have suggested this mystery can be solved by off-duty agents being present. The only known off-duty agent was James Powell of the 112th Intelligence Group. Powell's usual job was photographic surveillance of domestic dissidents like Oswald. Powell took a photograph of the open window and sniper's nest of boxes on the sixth floor of the Book Depository less than a minute after the shooting.

The motorcade was scheduled to leave Love Field airport at 11:30am. The drive through Dallas was expected to take 45 minutes, with the President arriving for a luncheon at 12:15pm. The motorcade was to pass through Dealey Plaza at around 12:10pm. However, the late arrival of Air Force One was compounded by the President spending more time with the crowd awaiting his arrival than predicted. JFK went to the people, pressing outstretched hands and being grabbed as if his touch would cure the sick as with the fabled prophets of old. The motorcade eventually moved away more than 15 minutes late.

It is impossible to determine conclusively where Lee Harvey Oswald was in the Texas School Book Depository (T.S.B.D.) between 12:00 and 12:32pm as the motorcade made its way toward his location. One witness places him in the TSBD's second-floor lunchroom as late as 12:25pm, making the alleged assassin seem nonchalant about his mission. Even discounting this testimony, Oswald seems unlikely to have been on the

ABOVE The last kiss of sun. In the final seconds prior to the assassination, President Kennedy takes in the adulation of the crowd. Nellie Connally, seen in front of the Kennedys with her husband, had just told JFK: "Mr. President, you can't say that Dallas doesn't love you."

sixth floor of the building before 12:20pm as his colleague Bonnie Ray Williams was there eating his lunch and saw no one.

The President's limousine was driven by Agent William Greer with Agent Roy Kellerman beside him. In front of John and Jackie Kennedy were Governor Connally and his wife Nellie. Senator Yarborough was originally meant to be in JFK's car until a row saw LBJ forced to have him in the Vice President's car.

There were thousands on the streets of downtown Dallas. It was a larger and more positive crowd than Kennedy had expected. Thousands of flyers featuring mug shots of JFK and proclaiming "Wanted For Treason" were distributed in Dallas on November 21. On the morning of November 22 the *Dallas Morning News* printed an ominous full-page ad, bordered in black like an obituary, attacking Kennedy as appeasing communism. When JFK saw it he said: "We're heading into nut country today." The ad was funded by a member of the Hunt oil dynasty.

As the motorcade came to the end of Houston Street, Nellie Connally turned to JFK, saying: "Mr. President, you can't say that Dallas doesn't love you." Kennedy beamed at her. They were probably the last words he heard.

It is this point in the route that provokes one of the biggest mysteries of the assassination. If Oswald was the lone shooter in the T.S.B.D., why did he not shoot Kennedy as the car moved slowly along Houston Street toward him? It provided a clearer shot and much more time.

It was 12:30pm as the motorcade turned onto Elm Street in front of the T.S.B.D. The first shot rang out. The Warren Commission thought this shot missed and caused the wound to witness James Tague. Others, including Governor Connally, believed the first shot hit JFK. To the majority of witnesses, there was a pause then they heard two more shots closer together.

On the film shot by witness Abraham Zapruder we can see Kennedy clutching at his throat and Governor Connally turning towards him. Connally is not injured. Turning to his other side, Connally was hit in the back, crying out: "Oh no, no, no. My God, they are going to kill us all."

Agent Kellerman shouted: "We're hit!" Instead of following standard procedure, Agent Greer hit the brakes, slowing the car. The third shot rang out, exploding President Kennedy's head.

Agent Clint Hill leapt from the running board of the follow-up car as Mrs. Kennedy climbed out onto the rear of the limo to retrieve a piece of her husband's head. As sirens erupted and the limousine sped towards Parkland Memorial Hospital, Jackie Kennedy said: "They have killed my husband. I have his brains in my hand."

As the motorcade sped away, many in the shocked crowd at Dealey Plaza dropped to the ground or sought out cover. Police rushed toward the grassy knoll to hunt the assassins that they thought were there. Police near the T.S.B.D. were alerted by members of the public who thought they had heard shots come from the building.

At 12:38pm the presidential limousine came to a halt outside the hospital. Mrs. Kennedy held her husband's body. Blood ran from his head onto her clothes and down her leg. She said: "They've murdered my husband. They've murdered my husband."

Clint Hill took off his jacket and leaned over the President's body. Turning to his colleagues, he announced: "He's dead."

Aftermath

Most of those in Dealey Plaza who heard the first shot thought it was a firecracker or a car backfiring. By the time they heard the second shot, they knew it was gunfire. As the President's head was carved open by a bullet, his brain exploding in a pink spray, the first screams came. Bill Newman, lying on the grass of the knoll and covering his son, beat his fists against the ground with frustration.

O f the Dealey Plaza witnesses I have personally spoken to, the one with greatest clarity was Associated Press photographer Ike Altgens. He told of shock stopping his finger when it should have captured the moment of Kennedy's death, and recounted the confusion and paralysis holding onlookers in the first few seconds after they saw their President shot.

Altgens said: "Everyone froze or hit the ground. There was a stillness. I took another picture. Then police and people were rushing up the grassy knoll on the north side of Elm. I followed. I thought they were going to get the guy who did it. I wanted a picture of him."

Patrolman Joe Smith was one of the first up the knoll. He had been alerted by shouts: "They are shooting the President from the bushes." Approaching the parking lot behind the knoll, he smelt gunpowder and found a man who identified himself as Secret Service. Later Smith and Police Chief Jesse Curry would both say the man was "bogus." Within minutes, dozens of officers were searching around the knoll.

Most witnesses in Dealey Plaza thought the shots came from the knoll, but others believed that they had come from the Dal-Tex building or the Texas School Book Depository. Patrolman Marion Baker thought he heard shots coming from that direction. Seeing pigeons flying from the T.S.B.D.,

he ran into it, followed by the building's manager Roy Truly. On the second floor they found Oswald drinking a Coke. If Oswald were the assassin, he would have had to stash his rifle, race down the stairs, and buy the Coke within 90 seconds of the last shot. Oswald left the T.S.B.D. at 12:35pm by the front entrance. Shortly afterward, police sealed the building, finding a rifle between a stack of boxes on the sixth floor at 1:22pm.

The empty presidential limousine sat outside Parkland hospital, its back seat covered in bone, brain, and blood. Later, LBJ would order the car to be cleaned and rebuilt, destroying vital evidence. Inside the hospital, Jackie Kennedy sat outside the emergency room, still wearing bloodstained gloves, parts of her husband's brain entwined in her bracelet.

The doctors attending Kennedy thought the damage to his throat was an entry wound and recorded the back of his head as missing. Even though JFK was dead, Jackie wanted him to have the last rites. When Father Oscar Huber attended at 12:50pm, he found the President was already dead, his

ABOVE Time unfrozen. Witnesses to the assassination tell of being paralyzed by the realization that they had just seen and heard the President being shot. As this moment of frozen time ended, many in the crowd at Dealey Plaza began rushing toward the grassy knoll—some because they thought they were fleeing to safety, some because they were running to catch the shooter.

ABOVE Empty testament. The presidential limousine lies empty at Parkland Memorial Hospital in the minutes after JFK had been rushed there. While it stood resting, vital forensic evidence was destroyed when orders were given to throw a bucket of water over the back of the vehicle to clear debris and blood.

body totally covered by a bloodied sheet, but he still performed the ritual. Doctors declared JFK dead at 1:00pm, allowing for it to seem as if he had still been alive when the rites were received.

At 12:35pm, FBI head J. Edgar Hoover called Robert F. Kennedy. The two men had a long-standing enmity. Hoover said: "The President's been shot." Before RFK could ask any questions, Hoover put the phone down. There was no element of empathy. RFK later said Hoover had enjoyed telling him.

At 1:26pm, LBJ left the hospital, returning to Air Force One. At 1:30pm, the official announcement of JFK's death was made. As the news spread from radios and TV across the country, a tsunami of shock and grief crashed through millions of people. The majority of Dallas held its head in shame. Even the usually bustling streets of Manhattan were eerily quiet. America became a nation of whispers.

Doctors, police, and a judge told Secret Service agents that under Texan law, they could not take JFK's body until an autopsy had been completed. One of the Secret Service agents said: "F*** you!" A praying priest was shoved aside as the agents forced their way out of the hospital. A fight started. Guns were pulled. Jackie Kennedy found herself fleeing beside her

husband's remains. The Secret Service-led group sped toward Air Force One, knowing they had just stolen the body.

Back on Air Force One, LBJ had been making calls, including to his stockbroker. When Jackie Kennedy and JFK's aides boarded with the body, LBJ told them Bobby Kennedy had suggested he take the Oath of Office before they left Texas. This was a lie.

At 2:38pm, LBJ's old friend Judge Sarah T. Hughes swore him in as 36th President of the United States. Johnson insisted Jackie Kennedy be fetched from a restroom and stand beside him. Jackie refused to change out of her bloodstained clothes. She told Lady Bird Johnson: "I want them to see what they have done to Jack." Ashen and bloodied, she witnessed the violent transfer of power.

ABOVE Bloody transition. Lyndon Johnson is sworn in as President of the United States aboard Air Force One less than three hours after JFK's murder. LBJ insisted that the traumatized, blood-stained Jackie Kennedy stand beside him during the ceremony while it was being photographed.

BELOW Evidence handling. A Dallas policeman at Police Headquarters holds up the rifle allegedly used to kill President Kennedy to show to journalists. The evidence recording and handling procedures used during the arrest and charging of Oswald were at best a bad joke, at worst criminal.

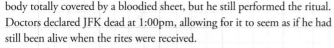

THE SIXTH FLOOR: EVIDENCE AGAINST OSWALD

In the aftermath of the assassination, television showed images of a Dallas detective holding aloft the rifle allegedly fired by Oswald. These did little to inspire belief that the local police investigation was a model of forensic scrutiny. The physical evidence paraded by Dallas police as recovered from the sixth floor of the T.S.B.D. has never convinced conspiriologists of Oswald's guilt. The police's best exhibits were a rifle without Oswald's fingerprints, a faulty scope, and three empty shell casings—one so dented it was unlikely to have been able to hold a bullet. However, the three shell casings were important to the Warren Commission's belief that Oswald fired three shots. In the 1990s, researcher Anna-Marie Kuhns-Walko found solid documentary evidence that only two shell casings were originally recovered from the T.S.B.D..

The Murder of Officer Tippit

The assassination of John F. Kennedy was not the only murder that took place in Dallas on November 22, 1963. Another slaying happened within an hour of JFK's death. Though less well known, the shooting of Dallas policeman J.D. Tippit is intrinsically linked to the events in Dealey Plaza.

The execution of J.D. Tippit was as cold and cruel as Kennedy's killing. It was this murder that Lee Harvey Oswald was first arrested for. Not surprisingly, the events surrounding it feature heavily in many conspiracy theories.

J.D. Tippit—whose initials stood for nothing in particular—was a World War II veteran and Bronze Star recipient. Married with three children, he had been a member of the Dallas police for 11 years by 1963.

Tippit's car—Dallas Police vehicle #10—could often be found parked outside the Dobbs House Restaurant. Two days before his own death, Tippit was in Dobbs when another regular customer began to curse over his order. Tippit shot a glance at the troublesome patron, but did nothing. In evidence to the Warren Commission, waitress Mary Dowling confirmed that the dissatisfied diner was Lee Harvey Oswald. She also confirmed that Tippit and Oswald knew each other, and that Jack Ruby also used Dobbs.

By 1:00pm on November 22, Oswald had returned to his boarding house. Shortly after, landlady Earlene Roberts saw "a police car stop directly in front. They sounded the horn, a kind of tit-tit—twice." She thought the car was numbered #107 and signaling Oswald: "They then drove away just before he came out." Roberts last saw Oswald at 1:04pm across the road waiting by a bus stop.

Between 1:11 and 1:14pm, Officer Tippit was driving slowly eastward on East 10th Street in the Oak Cliff area of Dallas. He was seen to pull alongside a man and exchange words before he opened his car door and began to walk around the front. At this point, officer Tippit was shot three times in the chest. After he had fallen to ground, a fourth shot was fired into his head, killing him.

Several witnesses saw the shooting and its aftermath. Later, some of these witnesses would identify Oswald as the killer. Tippit's fellow police officers were quickly informed of his shooting and a manhunt begun.

At around 1:35pm, shoe-store manager Johnny Brewer saw Oswald acting suspiciously in the doorway of his shop as police cars went by with sirens blazing. Brewer then followed Oswald to the Texas Theater cinema where he saw him sneak in. He alerted ticket seller Julie Pascal who called the police at 1:40pm.

At 1:50pm, more than two dozen policemen, sheriffs, and detectives arrived at the cinema to arrest Oswald for Tippit's killing. As detectives subdued Oswald, he repeatedly shouted: "I am not resisting arrest." As Oswald was punched and dragged out, Brewer heard a detective say: "Kill the President, will you." By 3:01pm, head of the FBI J. Edgar Hoover wrote a memo stating: "I called the Attorney General and told him I thought we had the man who killed the President down in Dallas."

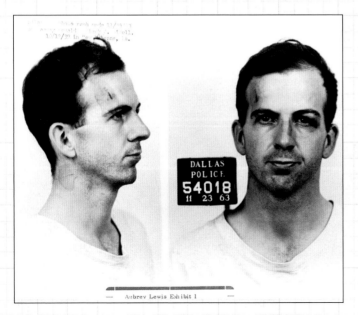

— Aubrey Lewis Exhibit 1 —

ABOVE Patrolman J.D. Tippitt, whose murder in Dallas on November 22, 1963 was the first crime Oswald was charged with. Strangely, Tippitt was nicknamed "JFK" by some of his colleagues who saw a physical resemblance between the two men.

LEFT America's Most Wanted—Dallas Police Department mug shots of Lee Harvey Oswald following his arrest for possible involvement in the John F. Kennedy assassination and the murder of Officer J.D. Tippit.

EMBARRASSING EVIDENCE

The physical evidence detailed by the Warren Commission in the Tippit shooting throws up some embarrassing issues for conspiracy debunkers. The Warren Commission claimed that Oswald left a light-colored jacket near the scene. The jacket was the wrong size for him, made in California, and contained dry-cleaning tags. Marina testified it was not his, and that Oswald had only two jackets, which were both Russian-made and never sent to a cleaners. Two of the shells recovered at the shooting were marked by policeman J.M. Poe with his initials. The shells later produced by the police and examined by the Commission were unmarked. Worse, Dallas Homicide-had stated that three of the bullets retrieved from Tippit were Westerns and one a Remington. However, the bullets given to the FBI for testing were actually two Westerns and two Remingtons.

It should be an open and shut case that Oswald killed Tippit, but not for conspiracy theorists. For a start, even the Warren Commission found it difficult to have Oswald walk to the scene of the shooting in the timeframe needed. The witness identifications of Oswald were highly flawed, as he was placed in line-ups visibly beaten, against Hispanics, teens, and men in suits. Also, several witnesses not called by the Warren Commission offered a different version of the shooting.

Frank Wright reported a man wearing a long coat who was not Oswald by Tippit's body, who drove away in car. Acquilla Clemons saw two men, neither of which were Oswald; after the shooting, one man waved to another with his gun, urging him to "go on!" Clemons was later interviewed by someone posing as a detective who told her "Someone might hurt me if I talked about what I saw."

Warren Reynolds, who chased the gunman, was not sure it was Oswald either. He was finally interviewed by the FBI in January 1964. Two days later he was shot in the head. A man called Darrell Garner was arrested, but a former Carousel Club dancer and friend of Jack Ruby, Betty Mooney MacDonald, gave him an alibi. Shortly afterward, MacDonald was arrested. Within an hour of her detention, she was found dead in her cell.

Officer J.D. Tippit was buried by his grieving family on November 25, 1963, the same day that Oswald and JFK were buried. Depending on which version you believe, he was the second victim of Oswald or the second victim of the conspiracy to kill Kennedy.

ABOVE The alleged gun and bullets used by Lee Harvey Oswald to kill Patrolman J.D. Tippit. However, far from being convincing proof of his guilt, some conspiriologists believe the bullets actually provide evidence Oswald did not kill Tippit.

BELOW How it happened? Dallas Police re-enact the alleged interaction between Lee Harvey Oswald and Officer Tippit before Tippit was killed. However, some witnesses claim to have seen two men involved in the murder, not just one.

The Shooting of Lee Harvey Oswald

The assassination of John F. Kennedy and its aftermath were followed by Americans watching flickering black-and-white live broadcasts from Dallas. Still reeling from the shock of the President's killing, they were not prepared for what they saw next—the brutal murder of the man that they expected to stand trial for the crime, live on television. However, from the moment Lee Harvey Oswald was apprehended for the murder of police officer J.D. Tippit, many things had seemed somewhat odd, somewhat wrong.

The first anomalous event in the apprehending, charging, and brutal death of Lee Harvey Oswald happened just 15 minutes after the shooting. At 12:45pm on Dallas Police radio, dispatcher Gerald Henslee gave out a description of the suspect wanted for killing Kennedy. Despite no one knowing who gave the description to the police inspector J.H. Sawyer and there being no reason to suspect Oswald at that point, the description matched him perfectly.

Within an hour of Oswald being dragged into the Homicide and Robbery Office at 2:02pm, Director of the FBI J. Edgar Hoover had written to his deputies claiming that they had the man who killed the President. At 4:58pm Dallas time, Air Force One touched down in Washington. Journalist Theodore H. White left the plane, reporting that President Johnson had already been briefed on Oswald's identity and that there was no conspiracy.

By 4:58pm, Oswald had not even been charged with Officer Tippit's murder, let alone the President's assassination. He had not been identified by any witnesses, nor fingerprinted. His wife had not been questioned, nor had any of the evidence later used against him—such as the photograph allegedly showing him with a rifle and pistol—been collected by this time.

It is understandable why many conspiracy researchers find this statement of certainty suspicious, especially as soon after his capture, Oswald told reporters in a hallway: "I didn't shoot anyone. They're taking me in because of the fact I lived in the Soviet Union. I'm just a patsy!" Not exactly statements negating a conspiracy.

The police held a midnight press conference. Dallas District Attorney Henry Wade briefed the press on what they knew of Oswald. In detailing his activities, Wade made the mistake of saying he was a member of the CIA-funded pro-Castro group Free Cuba Committee. A voice called out: "Henry, that's the Fair Play for Cuba Committee." The voice belonged to local nightclub owner and known Mafia associate Jack Ruby. None of the many Dallas police officers who knew him seemed to wonder why he was at the press conference or why he was an expert on pro-Castro groups.

As he was dragged away from the press conference, Oswald learnt from one of the reporters that he was being charged with Kennedy's killing. Oswald responded: "I have not been charged with that. In fact, nobody has said that to me yet. The first thing I heard about it was when the newspaper reporters in the hall asked me that question." Someone else called out to the obviously beaten prisoner: "How did you hurt your eye?" Oswald said: "A policeman hit me."

Given the seriousness of the crimes Oswald was accused of, you would expect copious notes of Oswald's hours of interrogation to have been taken by Captain William Fritz of Dallas Homicide and FBI special agents James

Bookhout and James Hosty. They told the Warren Commission that there were no notes, and no stenographic or tape recordings of the sessions. It later emerged that this was not the truth. During questioning, Oswald refused to admit to either killing, denied owning a rifle, claimed the rifle photo of him was fake, and claimed he knew nothing about the fake ID in the name A. J. Hidell. He refused all locally based legal representation, holding out for lawyers from the American Civil Liberties Union or Communist Party USA counsel John Abt.

On Sunday morning at 11:21am, more than 70 police officers were taking part in Oswald's transfer from the Dallas Police Headquarters

ABOVE Protective custody? Detectives escort Lee Harvey Oswald during his transfer, moments before he was shot. Given the public enmity toward Oswald, security procedures were suspiciously woeful.

OPPOSITE, ABOVE Justice denied. The fatal moment Jack Ruby shot Oswald, when many conspiracy theories were born. His actions denied America the chance to see justice done at a trial. Ruby's motivation and Mafia connection remain core elements of the assassination mystery.

OPPOSITE, BELOW Special FBI Agent James Hosty testifying before the House Judiciary Committee in December 1975 about the destruction of Oswald's note to him.

to the county jail. As the handcuffed prisoner was walked through the basement of the building in front of reporters and television cameras, a short, stocky man pushed out of the crowd, shoved his .38 revolver into Oswald's abdomen, and fired. That man was Jack Ruby.

Oswald was rushed to the Parkland Memorial Hospital—where Kennedy had been declared dead just two days earlier—but doctors could not save him. He was declared dead at 1:07pm.

With that one shot, Jack Ruby had turned all the odd elements of Oswald's detention into something flooded with suspicion. When Ruby shot Oswald, he did more than take a life—he stole America's chance to see justice being done. Live on television, Ruby's murderous act gave birth to a sense of conspiracy and left the millions of people watching asking two questions in bewilderment—who was Jack Ruby and why did he shoot Oswald?

OSWALD'S SECRET NOTE TO THE FBI

Two weeks before the assassination of JFK, Oswald walked into the Dallas FBI office and left a note for FBI Special Agent James Hosty. A fortnight later, Agent Hosty—who had been assigned to watch Oswald when he arrived in Texas—was with local police detectives questioning him about killing JFK. The existence of Oswald's note and the fact that the FBI removed Hosty's name and address from Oswald's notebook before submitting it to the Warren Commission did not become known until 1975. Hosty was officially reprimanded for misleading the Warren Commission, but maintained that his boss Gordon Shanklin had ordered him to burn Oswald's note in the wake of the assassination. Hosty always claimed that the note contained no more than a warning to him from Oswald to stop bothering his wife.

Jack Ruby

It is not hyperbole to call the assassination of JFK the most notorious murder in American history. Shimmering at the heart of this dark and complex murder mystery are two people—Lee Harvey Oswald and Jack Ruby. They are its visible players. If we can understand more of who they were, we may find clues to the conspiracy. Oswald and Ruby may be the only real guides we have to lead us through a shadowed labyrinth.

Before November 1963, Ruby had led a colorful if not distinguished life. Born as Jacob Rubenstein in Chicago in 1911, by the time he reached his early twenties he had been a salesman, a professional boxer, and errand runner for the small-time end of the Chicago Mob. After World War II and now going by the name of Jack Ruby, he moved to Dallas. By the late 1950s, he had opened the Carousel Club there.

The Carousel Club was the epitome of low-level sleaze. Ruby tried to apply a veneer of class to its burlesque and booze, but it was a gravity well for hard drinkers and men who wanted to stare at women's breasts. It attracted a large number of Dallas cops as patrons. Nancy Perrin Rich, who worked at the club, testified to the Warren Commission that Ruby ordered her to give free drinks to cops, stating: "There isn't a cop in Dallas that doesn't know Jack Ruby... they lived in his place."

Despite this, the Commission found no evidence that Ruby entered the basement to kill Oswald with police assistance. However, in 1979 the House Select Committee on Assassinations reported: "The Committee was troubled by unlocked doors along the stairway route and removal of security guards... There is evidence the Dallas Police Department withheld relevant information concerning Ruby's entry."

At his trial for Oswald's murder in 1964, Ruby first pled guilty, claiming he acted to spare Jackie Kennedy the pain of a trial. He then changed

JACK RUBY & SETH KANTOR - THE MINOR MOBSTER AND THE JOURNALIST

White House correspondent Seth Kantor was a passenger in the motorcade and found himself at Parkland Memorial Hospital in the aftermath of the shooting. Whilst there, Kantor ran into Jacky Ruby, an old acquaintance from his days on the *Dallas Times Herald*. The two spoke and Kantor testified to these facts to the Warren Commission. However, the Commission dismissed Kantor as mistaken. Despite knowing Ruby personally, he must have got it wrong. This was a convenient assumption for the Commission to make, especially as it negated suggestions Ruby was at the hospital planting a pristine bullet on a stretcher. Angered by his dismissal, Kantor went on to investigate Ruby, producing the book *Who Was Jack Ruby?* In 1979, the House Select Committee concluded that Kantor was probably not mistaken on his Parkland encounter with Ruby.

his plea to insanity, but was found guilty and sentenced to death. When interviewed by Chief Justice Earl Warren in June 1964, Ruby pleaded to be taken to Washington, saying: "I want to tell the truth and I can't tell it here... my life is in danger." Warren refused.

At the end of 1966, Ruby won the right to a new trial. On January 3, 1967, he died of cancer. Before his death, he claimed to have been injected with cancer. It was not the only conspiratorial statement he made. In his letters from prison, he urged people to read *A Texan Looks at Lyndon* (see The LBJ Conspiracy Theory, page 50,) saying: "It may open your eyes to a lot of things." He also told journalists: "Everything pertaining to what's happening has never come to the surface. The world will never know the true facts of what occurred, my motives. The people who had so much to gain, such an ulterior motive for putting me in the position I'm in, will never let the true facts come above board to the world."

FBI records suggest Ruby was involved in narcotics and had smuggled weapons into Cuba during the 1950s. In 1959, he was personally involved in attempts to free Mafia boss Santo Trafficante from prison in Cuba. While in jail, Ruby had said to a friend: "They're going to find out about Cuba. They're going to find out about the guns, find out about New Orleans, find out about everything." Telephone records show that

ABOVE Underbelly. Jack Ruby stands outside his club with two of his dancers. Ruby was more a face in the seedy underbelly of Dallas than a major figure in its underworld, but evidence shows he was connected to top-ranking Mafia figures.

OPPOSITE Full of secrets. Jack Ruby walks into a Dallas courtroom for sentencing after being found guilty of Oswald's murder. Although he died before he had a chance to talk in court, at his second trial it became clear Ruby was likely to spill the secrets he had kept during his original conviction.

LEFT From burlesque to bullets. Jack Ruby's Carousel Club was the sleazy nexus where Dallas cops rubbed shoulders and shared drinks with elements of the criminal class. Why Ruby went from peddling booze and breasts to firing bullets has to be one of the key concerns of any JFK conspiracy theory.

BELOW Gun control. The gun Jack Ruby used to kill Lee Harvey Oswald, thereby controling forever what the world would learn from the alleged assassin of President Kennedy.

before the assassination in 1963, Ruby spoke with both Trafficante and New Orleans Mafia boss Carlos Marcello.

The Warren Commission claimed that Ruby was not "part of any conspiracy" and that there was no "significant link between Ruby and organized crime." However, the Commission ignored a memo from its assistant counsels Burt Griffin and Leon Hubert, who wrote: "The most promising links between Jack Ruby and the assassination of President Kennedy are established through underworld figures and anti-Castro Cubans, and extreme right-wing Americans... on evidence available... Ruby was involved in illegal dealings with Cubans who might have had contact with Oswald."

The key question for many researchers is did Ruby know Oswald before the assassination? Rose Cheramie had claimed so. Secret Service Agent Roger Warner interviewed one of Ruby's strippers, Karen Bennett Carlin, who initially claimed Oswald visited the Carousel. He reported: "Mrs. Carlin was highly agitated... She stated to me that she was under the impression that Lee Harvey Oswald, Jack Ruby, and other individuals unknown to her were involved in a plot to assassinate President Kennedy." Robert F. Kennedy certainly believed Ruby and Oswald were connected, telling aide LaVern Duffy "It's impossible Oswald and Ruby didn't know each other."

A Country Reacts...
an Investigation Is Commissioned

Shock and grief can warp our lives like no other forces. All the usual assumptions of solidity and continuance are suspended. We enter an alien, frightening world where certainty has been ripped from us.

ABOVE United States of Grief. Jacqueline and Caroline Kennedy kneel beside President John F. Kennedy's flag-draped coffin as he lies in state at the Capitol Rotunda, Washington, DC.

The six seconds that killed Kennedy caused a manifestation of shock and grief across the U.S. unlike anything since the assassination of Abraham Lincoln nearly a century before. However, Lincoln's murder was not an event of the television age. The modern mass media allowed America to observe and commune in collective grief in a way no nation had experienced before.

In the first minutes, as the news interrupted normal programing—and normal life—shock rolled across the nation. Traffic halted and drivers stopped in disbelief as word spread from car to car like contagion. Schools closed. People congregated in bars to watch the news together. They went to churches and prayed. Both women and men were seen openly weeping in the street. By the evening, more than 75 percent of the nation was collectively watching the Dallas horror story unfold in black and white.

There was no pre-arranged plan for a State funeral for a slain president. Despite her grief or possibly because of it, Jackie Kennedy threw herself into arranging one. Modeling her husband's funeral on that of Lincoln, JFK's body was first put in repose in the East Room of the White House. Still in the bloodstained clothes she had refused to change, Mrs. Kennedy finally left her husband's body with a Marine honor guard and two Catholic priests. Newly created President Johnson came to pay his respects, as did former Presidents Truman and Eisenhower.

On the Sunday afternoon, 300,000 people lined the streets to watch a horse-drawn caisson take Kennedy to lie in state below the Capitol Rotunda. Johnson issued Presidential Proclamation 3561, declaring Monday a national day of mourning. Foreign leaders and dignitaries flew to Washington. When the caisson took Kennedy on his final journey to Arlington National Cemetery, the world was watching.

Across the globe, people mourned. U.S. intelligence recorded that even in the Soviet Union, church bells tolled for Kennedy. However, as the tributes were given in almost every nation, as JFK's former enemies at home rushed to praise him, questions began to be asked. How? Why? One lone gunman?

In the Soviet Union, the CIA discovered the Politburo (the Communist executive body) believed the assassination was the result of "an ultra-right coup." They feared it presaged an attack on Cuba or East Germany. But for President Johnson, it was questions in America that gave him headaches.

Johnson originally wanted the Texas authorities to hold an enquiry, but fear of public reaction led him to lean on the Dallas Police, via the FBI, to stop them referring to Oswald as a Marxist. With Senator James Eastland threatening to investigate as well as several congressmen and senators calling for a public enquiry, LBJ panicked, curtailing open scrutiny.

On November 24, J. Edgar Hoover stated in a memo to LBJ's aide Walter Jenkins: "The thing I am concerned about, and so is Mr. Katzenbach [Deputy Attorney General], is having something issued so we can convince the public Oswald is the real assassin." Katzenbach replied on November 25: "Speculation about Oswald's motivations ought to cut off, and we should have some basis for rebutting the thought it was a Communist or a right-wing conspiracy."

LBJ's solution was to form the President's Commission on the Assassination of President Kennedy on November 27. It became known as the Warren Commission, after its chairman, Chief Justice Earl Warren. LBJ had to cajole Warren into the assignment, reminding him of his "patriotic duty." Commission member Senator Richard Russell only agreed to participate after LBJ bullied him and warned him of direct Soviet/Cuban threats to the U.S. if the Commission was unable to convince the public there was no conspiracy. Other members of the seven-man committee such as Representative Gerald Ford, former President of the World Bank John J. McCloy, and former head of the CIA Allen Dulles, needed no cajoling.

Years later, McCloy would be accused of having been at a meeting in Texas with LBJ, J. Edgar Hoover, and oil barons such as H.L. Hunt and Clint Murchison Sr. when they discussed getting rid of Kennedy. Dulles had been fired as CIA chief for lying to Kennedy over the Bay of Pigs. His deputy and friend Charles P. Cabell was fired at the same time. His brother Earle Cabell was Mayor of Dallas on the day of the assassination. To conspiriologists, with some members of the Commission possibly linked to any conspiracy, there was never any doubt what the result of its investigation would be.

JAMES EASTLAND'S COMMUNIST CONSPIRACY

One of the great ironies of the Warren Commission is that it worked so hard to prove there was no conspiracy, yet it had partly come into being because of one politician who believed Kennedy's death was a plot. Senator James Eastland, a Democrat from Mississippi, was a virulent proponent of racial segregation and a rabid anti-communist. President Johnson said of him: "Jim Eastland could be standing right in the middle of the worst Mississippi flood ever, and he'd say the niggers caused it, helped out by the Communists." Eastland's hunch was that Oswald's communist connections meant there was a conspiracy to kill Kennedy. As Chairman of the Internal Security Subcommittee, Eastland had the Washington clout to cause all sorts of problems if his threats to have his committee investigate had materialized, so he had to be appeased.

The Warren Commission and its Inconvenient and Missing Witnesses

On November 23, 1963, the streets of Dallas were pulsing, crowded with people. However, Dealey Plaza was toward the end of the President's route. There were fewer people. Fewer witnesses. It was almost as if someone had designed the fateful moments of history about to unfold with as few observers as possible.

However, there were some eyes on this nexus point in history, dozens who saw the brutal disruption of order and witnessed the assassination. Even more saw something of its aftermath as people surged up the grassy knoll and police began hunting for possible shooters.

Many more had seen some element leading up to the murder or had known key people such as Oswald or Ruby. As the Warren Commission found out, one thing the crime of the twentieth century did not lack was witnesses. The problem for the Commission was that many of them were saying inconvenient things. In fact, if the evidence of some witnesses was to be believed, there is absolutely no way the Commission's conclusion that Oswald acted alone was sustainable.

As government memos show, the Warren Commission was partly created to ensure that the public was "satisfied Oswald was the assassin; that he did not have confederates who are still at large." This may explain why its approach to witnesses seemed to be highly selective. As soon as its report was printed, allegations emerged that it had rewritten witness testimony, bullied witnesses, and ignored witnesses offering evidence suggestive of any conspiracy.

The Commission did not interview obvious witnesses such as Mary Moorman, who took one of the best-positioned photographs of the assassination and who heard more than three shots. The Commission never contacted Bill and Gayle Newman, who watched the motorcade with their children from the grassy knoll's northern edge. This might have been because they were so convinced shots were coming from behind them that they flung their children down and fell on top of them.

Witnesses complained of only being able to tell the Commission what it wanted to hear. Phillip Willis, who thought there was a grassy knoll shooter, was not questioned on his opinion that the shot which "took the president's skull off came from the right front." Some witnesses complained of evidence tampering. Orville Nix, who initially believed shots came from the grassy knoll, claimed the film he took that day was

---

ABOVE Duck and cover. The sheltering love of Bill and Gayle Newman, who threw themselves down when they thought they heard shots coming from behind them on the grassy knoll, is evident in this shot. However, the Warren Commission ignored their testimony on the direction of the shots they heard.

THE BULLET THAT MISSED

Traffic generated by JFK's motorcade caused James Tague to stop his car close to the edge of the Triple Underpass. Suddenly he heard a shot, then another. As he heard a third shot, something stung him on the face. He thought the shots came from the knoll. After the shooting, Detective Buddy Walthers saw blood on Tague's cheek where debris had fired up after a bullet hit the kerb. The scarred kerb and Tague's evidence led the Commission to conclude that one of Oswald's shots had missed, leading to the "magic bullet" theory, that one bullet caused JFK's neck wound and all the wounds to Connally before emerging almost pristine. Forensic analysis showed that the kerb had been hit by a bullet with no copper, unlike the bullets allegedly fired by Oswald. The FBI later destroyed this evidence. The scarred stone was patched with foreign material before being placed in the National Archives—no authorization was ever given for this.

ABOVE Cover-up. Even physical evidence such as the physically scarred kerb proving there was a shot that missed has been tampered with. The bullet damage to the kerb was mysteriously covered up by foreign material before it was sent to the National Archives.

LEFT Polaroid moment. Mary Moorman's fifth Polaroid photograph taken during the assassination. Despite being one of the best-placed witnesses, as her photos show, she was not called to give testimony to the Warren Commission.

not identical to the one he received back from the FBI. Witness Jean Hill even claimed her recorded evidence to the Commission was fabricated.

Some witnesses claimed they were intimidated. Marina Oswald, held by the Secret Service until her testimony to the Commission, was threatened with losing her children. Richard Carr saw a heavy-set man with horn-rimmed glasses and a tan sports coat on the sixth floor of the depository. After the shooting he followed the man until he was picked up by a Nash stationwagon. An FBI agent told Carr: "If you didn't see Lee Harvey Oswald in the Depository with a rifle, you didn't see it." Carr received threatening phone calls telling him to leave Texas. He found dynamite taped to his car ignition. Carr was not called by the Warren Commission, but when he testified at the trial of Clay Shaw, who was charged as being involved in a conspiracy to kill JFK, a gunman attempted to kill him.

The Warren Commission was unable to question some of the most important eyes on history, as the FBI was not able to trace them. Now known to researchers as "Babushka Lady" thanks to her headscarf, one woman is visible in photographs filming events as she stands between Elm and Main Street. In 1970, Beverly Oliver, a former Carousel Club burlesque artist, claimed she was Babushka Lady. Her story is not generally believed and the true identity of the covered woman and why she and the images she took were never found remains a mystery.

A man who unfurled his umbrella as the motorcade approached is seen in several photographs. The fact that no umbrella was needed that day has led conspiriologists to speculate that "Umbrella Man" was giving a signal to assassins. In 1978, Louie Witt claimed he had used the umbrella as a way of heckling JFK. Witt's story is flawed and many doubt he was Umbrella Man. No one has come forward to claim to be the "Dark-Complected Man" seen with Umbrella Man, and who in some frames appears to be using a walkie-talkie and giving a salute.

Some of the evidence most dissonant to the Commission's conclusions comes from one of its most high-profile witnesses—Governor John Connally. He stated, "I'll never change my opinion: the first bullet hit the President, I was hit by the second bullet, the third bullet did not hit me, but hit the President." As the Commission concluded one bullet had missed the car completely and their timings meant Oswald could not have fired four shots, this implied there had to be a second shooter.

RIGHT Mystery men. Are "Umbrella Man" and "Dark-Complected Man" innocent bystanders to history or signaling for the shooting to begin? In later years, Louie Witt claimed to be holding the umbrella in this photo, but no one has come forward to admit to being the man making the strange hand gesture.

The Zapruder Film

The Zapruder film of 486 frames totaling 26.6 seconds is possibly the most important and debated amateur movie in history. Despite the contentious life of the film since November 22, 1963, what was captured on Kodachrome II 8mm color is regarded as the most complete visual record of the assassination of JFK.

It was an essential part of the evidence considered by the Warren Commission. More than that, its images dominate how we remember the assassination. Our visual view of that fateful day comes largely from the point of view of Zapruder's camera.

Abraham Zapruder was a 58-year-old businessman when the film he shot turned his surname into one synonymous with the killing of Kennedy. Of Russian-Jewish extraction, in 1954 Zapruder founded a fashion company that he headquartered in the Dal-Tex building across the street from the Texas School Book Depository.

Zapruder had not originally planned to film the President's motorcade, but his secretary Lillian Rogers persuaded him to make a 14-mile round trip home to collect his top-of-the-line Bell & Howell Zoomatic camera. Half an hour before the motorcade arrived, he went down into Dealey Plaza with his receptionist Marilyn Sitzman to find a spot from which to film. Zapruder picked a concrete plinth on Elm Street next to the grassy knoll and close to the Triple Underpass.

Unlike others that day, when the shots happened, he kept the camera to his eye. Even when Zapruder was screaming: "They've killed him! They've killed him!" he kept the camera rolling, capturing Jackie Kennedy's attempts to climb out of the vehicle. His film shows the presidential limousine turning onto Elm Street, following it until the underpass. He caught the fatal shot to JFK's head when the limousine was almost in front of and just below him. At the time, Zapruder thought the shots came from behind him.

After the assassination, Zapruder went back to his office and sent his secretary to find a Secret Service agent. By 6:30pm on November 22, Zapruder had the original film and one copy, while the Secret Service had two copies. Later that night, Zapruder was contacted by *Life* magazine, which wanted to buy the film. The next day, all rights to the film were sold for $150,000 (more than $1 million in current terms).

The November 29 issue of *Life* used 30 frames of the film. Other frames were featured in later editions, but the next major use of the film was as black and white frames for the Warren Commission—Exhibit 885. The Zapruder film became the backbone around which the Commission had to fit much of the other evidence. However, the frames used were selective and contained errors made while being copied. Investigators' inability to view and reproduce the full film caused consternation and suspicion.

The first public showing of the film took place when it was subpoenaed by Jim Garrison and shown as part of Clay Shaw's trial in 1969. It was

ABOVE Shooting down the "magic bullet" theory. Frame 273 of Zapruder's film appears to show an unharmed Governor Connally turning in concern toward the President. If that is correct, it destroys the timings for the Warren Commission's single bullet theory.

LEFT Capturing history. The Bell & Howell Zoomatic camera used by Abraham Zapruder to capture the brutal unfolding of history. The camera is now kept at the U.S. National Archives.

not until 1975, when ABC's *Good Night America* broadcast the film, that the American public got to see it. When they did, there was shock and outrage. Many viewed its capture of Kennedy's head moving back and to the left as confirmation that the fatal shot was not fired from the T.S.B.D. The huge uproar caused by seeing the Zapruder film played a big role in the establishing of the House Select Committee on Assassinations investigation in 1976.

Even though the film is now in the public archive, it remains controversial. Many researchers do not accept it as authentic. While the majority do believe it to be genuine, its completeness is still disputed. Experts Max Holland and Johann Rush made a careful study of the film and concluded that there was a significant pause between frame 132 and 133. If this is right, it means a possible first shot was missed out. Other researchers and scientific experts have concluded frames have been removed.

Not only is Zapruder's film subject to allegation after allegation, but Abraham Zapruder himself became the subject of conspiracy theories. After his death in 1970, anti-Semitic theories proclaiming him a "32nd degree Master Mason" and member of a "pro-Jewish CIA cabal linked to the Dallas Council on World Affairs" began to circulate. No hard evidence was offered for these claims.

However, researcher Bruce Campbell Adamson began to investigate Zapruder's background. He uncovered the curious coincidence that before 1954, Zapruder worked at fashion company Nardis when it also employed the mother of LBJ's secretary Marie Fehmer, as well as Jeanne LeGon, future wife of Oswald's friend and CIA asset George de Mohrenschildt. Whether that makes Zapruder anything other than a man who just happened to point his camera at history is entirely open to interpretation.

ABOVE RIGHT Life exploded, life extinguished. The infamous pink explosion captured in frame 313 was originally suppressed at the express wish of Abraham Zapruder.

BELOW Defining recollection. The blurs in time forever frozen by the lens of Zapruder have defined the images of the assassination we all hold in our heads. However, they also raise many questions for which there are no definite answers. Why is Jackie crawling out of the car? Escape? To pick up a fragment of her husband's skull?

ZAPRUDER'S NIGHTMARE

On the night of November 22, Abraham Zapruder had the first of many assassination-related nightmares. In it, he found himself wandering in New York's Times Square, a place screaming with neon and advertising. He came to a newspaper booth whose signs read: "SEE THE PRESIDENT'S HEAD EXPLODE!" When he woke, Zapruder felt chastened and worried. He still went ahead with the sale of the rights of his film, but made two key decisions. The first was to give $25,000 (more than $175,000 in 2012 terms) from the sale directly to the widow and grieving family of slain Dallas police officer J.D. Tippit. The other was to stipulate as a condition of sale that *Life* could not print frame 313 in the hope of sparing others the horror he had experienced.

The Warren Report Findings

On September 24, 1964, less than a year after it had been established, the Warren Commission delivered its 888-page final report to President Johnson. Three days later it was made public. Its conclusions were unambiguous—it found that Oswald acted alone and that neither he nor Jack Ruby was "part of any conspiracy, domestic or foreign, to assassinate President Kennedy."

The report also found that Oswald killed Tippit, and concluded that at the assassination "there were three shots fired" and "the same bullet which pierced the President's throat also caused Governor Connally's wounds." It determined there was "no evidence of conspiracy, subversion, or disloyalty to the U.S. Government by any Federal, State, or local official."

Right from the start, some Commission members such as Chief Justice Earl Warren and Senator Richard Russell, both of whom had been bullied into taking part, were worried that the Commission would end up just causing more controversy about the killing. However, Allen Dulles, Commission member and former CIA Director sacked by JFK, dismissed such concerns. His view was: "Nobody reads. Don't believe people read in this country. There will be a few professors… the public will read very little." Ultimately, Warren and Russell were proved right.

Even before publication of its finding, the Warren Commission was under attack. Lawyer and activist Mark Lane was one of the first to challenge the Commission. He asked it to let him represent the interests of Lee Harvey Oswald. They refused, appointing Walter E. Craig. Unfortunately for Oswald's interests, Craig represented them by not attending hearings, not cross-examining any witnesses, and not naming witnesses of his own.

While the Commission was sitting, Lane published an article detailing discrepancies in witness testimony, the failure of the paraffin test to prove Oswald had fired a gun, and testimony from doctors at Parkland Memorial

ABOVE The great and the good? The members of the Warren Commission (L–R): Rep. Gerald R. Ford (R, Mich.); Rep. Hale Boggs (D, Ala.); Sen. Richard B. Russell (D, Ga.); Supreme Court Chief Justice Earl Warren, Chairman; Sen. John S. Cooper (R, Ky.); global banker John J. McCloy; former head of the CIA Allen W. Dulles; J. Lee Rankin, Chief Counsel.

Hospital suggesting bullets had hit Kennedy from the front. In the United Kingdom, the article led to the formation of a Who Killed Kennedy Committee. Its members included Members of Parliament, historians, and Nobel Prize-winner Bertrand Russell.

In 1964, Bertrand Russell published a stinging attack on the Commission's conclusion entitled *16 Questions on the Assassination*. In it Russell stated: "The official version has been so riddled with contradictions it has been rewritten no less than three times. Blatant fabrications have received widespread coverage by the mass media, but denials of these same lies have gone unpublished. Photographs, evidence and affidavits have been doctored out of recognition. Some of the most important aspects of the case against Lee Harvey Oswald have been completely blacked out. Meanwhile, the F.B.I., the police and the Secret Service have tried to silence key witnesses or instruct them what evidence to give. Others involved have disappeared or died in extraordinary circumstances."

Among Bertrand Russell's 16 questions were: "Why were all the members of the Warren Commission closely connected with the U.S. Government? If, as we are told, Lee Harvey Oswald was the lone assassin, where is the issue of national security? If the Government is so certain

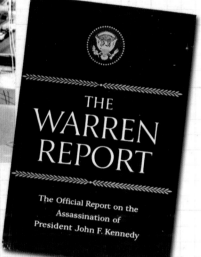

of its case, why has it conducted all its inquiries in the strictest secrecy? Why was the President's route changed at the last minute to take him past Oswald's place of work? Why has the medical evidence concerning the President's death been altered out of recognition?"

Attacks on the findings of the Warren Commission did not stop there. In 1966 two groundbreaking books were published attacking the Warren Commission conclusions. These were Mark Lane's *Rush to Judgement,* which went onto the bestseller list, and *Inquest: The Warren Commission and the Establishment of Truth* by investigative journalist Edward Jay Epstein. Both books destabilized any confidence in the idea of Oswald being a lone gunman. These books, plus the pioneering work of other researchers, put before the public evidence and key questions that the Warren Commission had completely failed to address.

The authority of the Warren Commission conclusions was further damaged in the public eye by the Clay Shaw trial in 1969, but worse was to come. Commission member Thomas Hale Boggs had only reluctantly signed off the report, believing J. Edgar Hoover had lied about the FBI's

relationship with Oswald. Boggs had always dissented on the single bullet theory and in 1972 was telling friends in Washington of his growing concerns about the assassination.

On October 16, 1972, the plane on which Hale Boggs and fellow Representative Nick Begich were traveling disappeared during its flight across Alaska. Neither the plane nor any bodies were ever found. The *Los Angeles Star* reported that at the time of his death "Boggs had startling revelations on Watergate and the assassination of President Kennedy." Reports such as this, hinting at a grand conspiracy, showed more than anything how badly the findings of the Warren Commission had failed to convince the public that Oswald had acted alone.

DOUBTING COMMISSIONERS

The alleged quip to Hale Boggs from Allen Dulles about releasing evidence—"Go ahead and print it, nobody will read it anyway"—was a strong possibility, as originally only 1,000 copies of the Commission's report were published. There was not even an index to the 15 volumes; it had to be created by conspiracy researchers. Within a decade of the report being released, four out of the seven members of the Commission—a majority—expressed doubt on its conclusions. Commission member Richard Russell eventually said: "No one man could have done the known shooting." Even the once-steadfast defender of the Commission's conclusions, member and future President Gerald Ford, eventually admitted that the CIA had hidden and destroyed information that "can easily be misinterpreted as collusion in JFK's assassination."

The Assassination of RFK

In the years after the slaying of his brother, Robert F. Kennedy saw America become a darker place. By 1968, it was a country dealing with the storm clouds of division on Vietnam, race, and poverty. Under the shadow of this brooding political weather, violence and protest in American streets had become commonplace. Many observers felt that the States were not united, but rather tearing themselves apart.

LOS ANGELES

A t the beginning of 1968, Bobby Kennedy had no plans to challenge President Johnson for the Democratic Presidential Nomination in the upcoming election. However, journalist Pete Hamill sent him a letter telling him he had seen pictures of RFK on poor people's walls and Kennedy had an "obligation of staying true to whatever it was that put those pictures on those walls."

Spurred on by the letter and LBJ's clear vulnerability, on March 16, RFK stood in the Caucus Room of the old Senate building and declared his candidacy. It was the same room that his brother had used for the same purpose eight years before. RFK said: "I run because I am convinced that this country is on a perilous course and because I have such strong feelings about what must be done. I feel that I'm obliged to do all I can."

Standing on a radical platform of racial and economic justice, ending aggressive foreign policies, and decentralizing power, Kennedy's campaign caught on with the young, the poor, and those suffering from injustice. On March 31, LBJ announced he would not stand for re-election. On April 4, Martin Luther King, Jr. was assassinated and reactive riots broke out in over 100 cities. This made RFK's campaign more emblematic of hope than ever before. However, it did not please everyone. FBI Director J. Edgar Hoover's deputy and probable lover Clyde Tolson told people: "I hope someone shoots and kills that son of a bitch."

On the night of June 5, Clyde Tolson got his wish. Fresh from celebrating his win in the California Primary, Bobby Kennedy was walking through the kitchen of the Ambassador Hotel in Los Angeles. A 24-year-old Palestinian immigrant, Sirhan Sirhan, ran in front of RFK and fired eight shots in his direction.

ABOVE Victory—Senator Robert Kennedy addresses the jubilant crowd, with his wife Ethel beside him, after winning the key California Primary. RFK had no way of knowing that instead of becoming closer to the presidency, he was just moments from his own murder.

BELOW The death of hope. Bobby Kennedy lies crumpled on the floor of the Ambassador Hotel. Kneeling beside him is 17-year-old Juan Romero, a busboy in the hotel, who placed a rosary in the hand of the dying man.

MANCHURIAN MIND-CONTROL PUPPET?

One of JFK's favorite novels, according to Frank Sinatra and others, was the 1959 thriller *The Manchurian Candidate* by Richard Condon. The book is about a communist, mind-controlled assassin unwittingly at work in the U.S. Elements of the book reflected the real CIA mind-control programs ARTICHOKE and MK-ULTRA. Even the pioneering hypnotist involved with these programs, William Joseph Bryan, publicly stated: "Sirhan was likely operating under some form of posthypnotic suggestion." Bryan, who got the alleged Boston Strangler Albert DeSalvo to confess to multiple homicides under hypnosis, also worked as a consultant for the movie of *The Manchurian Candidate*. Top experts in hypnotism such as Dr. Herbert Spiegel, former Clinical Professor of Psychiatry at Columbia College, looked at Sirhan's case and backed that initial offhand insight by Bryan. Strangely, Sirhan's notebooks are full of stream-of-consciousness writing that makes reference to DeSalvo.

Bobby collapsed on the floor. Sirhan was tackled by Olympic athlete Rafer Johnson, pro-football star Rosey Grier, and security man Bill Barry. They reported Sirhan as being possessed of superhuman strength, fighting them off to try firing his now-empty gun again.

Kennedy lay dying. He asked: "Is everybody safe, OK?" Turning his head, he gave a look of recognition to his wife Ethel. Then he closed his eyes and lost consciousness. He died 26 hours later.

As America watched the funeral of another slain Kennedy, no one immediately thought of a conspiracy as there were witnesses and a living shooter in custody. However, it soon became clear that RFK's murder was anything but straightforward and evidence was discovered suggesting that the assassination was most definitely a conspiracy.

Analysis of audiotape of the shooting shows 13 shots being fired. Sirhan's gun only held eight. Further analysis showed some of the shots coming too close together to have been fired from the same gun, proving there had been two shooters. Forensic evidence showed the shot that killed Kennedy was fired point blank behind his ear, no more than three inches away. In fact all the shots that hit Kennedy came from behind. At no point was Sirhan behind Kennedy and never closer to him than five feet away.

Two bullets were removed from RFK, five from other victims, and the Los Angeles Police Department placed one bullet as lost in the ceiling. Sirhan could only have fired eight times, but photos show further bullet holes in a doorframe in which at least one more bullet was embedded. Strangely, the doorframe was removed by police and subsequently lost.

Apart from Sirhan, the only other person at the murder scene holding a .22 pistol was security guard Thane Cesar, who was behind Kennedy. Confronted with witness testimony that he had been seen drawing a gun, Cesar said he had sold his .22 before the assassination. This turned out to be inaccurate. He sold it afterward.

During Sirhan's confession after the shooting, some detectives thought he showed signs of being hypnotized. At trial, the judge did not accept his confession. Sirhan claims to have no memory of the shooting, a claim which has stopped numerous parole applications.

RFK's brother Ted Kennedy gave the eulogy at his funeral, saying: "As my brother said many times, in many parts of this nation, to those he touched and who sought to touch him: 'Some men see things as they are and say why. I dream things that never were and say why not.'"

With those words, RFK, and maybe the last great American hope for a better future, was buried.

ABOVE Laurence Harvey stars as the brainwashed killer designed to enforce a sinister conspiracy in the 1962 film version of *The Manchurian Candidate*.

BELOW Killer or just another patsy? Unlike Oswald, Sirhan Sirhan survived police custody, but questions remain over his alleged role in the shooting of Bobby Kennedy.

Jim Garrison Investigates

Between April and September 1963, Lee Harvey Oswald was in New Orleans. Even to a conspiracy sceptic, his time in the Big Easy comes across as odd. Oswald, the pro-Castro pro-Communist who founded a one-man branch of Fair Play for Cuba, worked for a company owned by a noted anti-Castro campaigner, getting into public fights with anti-Castro Cuban exiles and even appearing on a television debate on the subject.

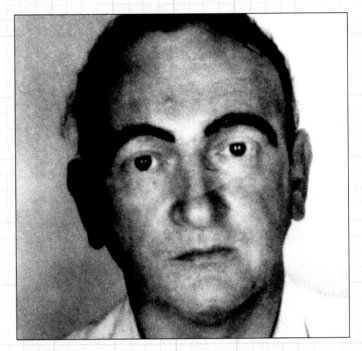

However, as shown by the address on leaflets Oswald gave out, he did this working from the same building—544 Camp Street—used by the extremist anti-Castro group the Cuban Revolutionary Council. Private investigator Guy Banister, a right-wing extremist and associate of the Cubans, used the same building. Information on Oswald in New Orleans was passed to District Attorney Jim Garrison. He also learned of accusations that Banister and David Ferrie, a pilot with links to mobster Carlos Marcello and extreme anti-Castroists, were involved in the plot to kill Kennedy.

Garrison investigated these claims and passed the information to the FBI, who questioned Ferrie twice before releasing him. Garrison did not pursue the matter until 1966 when Louisiana Senator Russell Long told him "Those fellows on the Warren Commission were dead wrong." This led Garrison to read all the Warren Commission evidence. Finding it woefully sloppy and contradictory, and the conclusion that Oswald had been a lone gunman untenable, Garrison secretly reopened his investigation.

Garrison became convinced that Banister, Ferrie, and a group of anti-Castro Cubans had been involved in gunrunning with CIA assistance. He also believed that he could prove that this combination was directly linked to Oswald and had been behind the assassination. The final piece of Garrison's puzzle was New Orleans businessman Clay Shaw. Garrison believed that Shaw worked for the CIA, and knew Ferrie and Oswald. He also believed that using the alias Clay Bertrand, Shaw had contacted lawyer Dean Andrews asking him to represent Oswald whilst he was in custody in Dallas.

Banister had died of a heart attack in 1964 and a week after news of Garrison's investigation became public in February 22, 1967, David Ferrie was found dead of a suspected aneurism in his apartment alongside two unsigned suicide notes. Before his death, Ferrie had telephoned an aide of Garrison, saying: "You know what this news story does to me, don't you. I'm a dead man. From here on, believe me, I'm a dead man." A week later, Garrison arrested Clay Shaw, charging him with conspiring to assassinate President Kennedy.

News of this gained Garrison international publicity, but also antagonism and ridicule from the press as well as elements of State and Federal government. When Shaw eventually faced trial on January 29, 1969, it seemed to many that all Garrison could present firm evidence of was that Shaw and Ferrie were part of the underground homosexual scene and that Ferrie and Oswald had known each other. The credibility of Garrison's case was further weakened at the trial when it emerged that the testimony of key witness Perry Russo had been obtained using hypnotism and the "truth serum" sodium pentothal. On March 1, 1969, the jury found Shaw not guilty.

It was an unequivocal defeat for Garrison's conspiracy theory involving Shaw. However, some vindication for Garrison was achieved in 1979: Richard Helms, a former CIA director, admitted that Clay had worked for the agency. In 1992, the judge at the trial, Edward Haggerty, said "I think Shaw put a good con job on the jury."

Garrison remains a divisive figure in JFK conspiracy research. To many he was crazy, crooked, or at best completely confused. To others, he was

ABOVE Dead men tell no tales. The police mug shot of David Ferrie. As soon as news of Garrison's investigation became public, Ferrie accurately predicted that he would be a "dead man." His death ended one of Garrison's most interesting lines of enquiry.

LEFT Conspiracy crusader. District Attorney Jim Garrison announcing to the press that the assassination conspiracy trial of Clay Shaw would start on January 21, 1969, the day after Richard Nixon was sworn in as President.

RIGHT New Orleans Noir. The life story of private investigator Jack Martin reads like something out of a 1930s detective novel. However, most of his at one-time seemingly outrageous claims about David Ferrie and Guy Bannister proved correct.

BELOW Innocent cleared of conspiracy. Flanked by two of his supporters through the trial, Clay Shaw holds up the newspaper headline which celebrates his being found not guilty of being involved in a conspiracy to kill President Kennedy. It took the jury just 54 minutes to find him innocent.

a true American hero—the man who saw something was deeply wrong and fought against the power of the secret state to expose it, whatever the personal cost.

Despite the Clay Shaw trial being the focus of Oliver Stone's movie *JFK*, few conspiriologists believe he was part of a plot to kill Kennedy. However, even those dismissing Garrison as a publicity-seeking oddball usually agree that he changed the climate for conspiracy research. Opinion polls showed that 20 percent less of the American public accepted the Warren Commission conclusions after the trial. Garrison not only promoted JFK's death as a conspiracy to the mainstream and brought about the first public viewing of the Zapruder film; he did it as an elected official unafraid to point the finger at elements of his own government.

After five decades, Garrison's investigation and the trial he brought remains the only time the American judicial system has attempted to prove there was a conspiracy to kill John F. Kennedy; and the only time the judicial system has tried to get justice for the slain president and expose the stolen history that had been denied the American people. In the end, it is this that is most remembered about Garrison's investigation, and not the failure to convict Clay Shaw.

JACK S. MARTIN

On the day that JFK was killed, low-rent private investigator Jack Martin was hospitalized after being pistol-whipped by his boss, fellow private investigator and former FBI agent Guy Banister. This violent act led to Martin telling police that Banister and David Ferrie had been involved in a conspiracy to kill Kennedy. The FBI contacted Martin on November 25, 1963, but dismissed him as unreliable. Martin's reputation for unreliability may be why Garrison once denied he was a source of information used to investigate Banister and Ferrie. After all, Garrison had called Martin an "undependable drunk." However, despite Martin's resemblance to a character from a seedy pulp novel, his claim that Oswald knew Ferrie was proved correct, as were his claims that Banister acted for Mafia boss Carlos Marcello and was involved with anti-Castro Cuban exiles.

Witnesses—the Trail of Death

Did the shots in Dealey Plaza end up taking more than just JFK's life? Is there a trail of death leading away from the assassination? Conspiracy researchers note that many key witnesses to the assassination and possible subsequent cover-up died in unusual circumstances.

Witnesses also seemed to conveniently die around periods of official enquiry. There were clusters of fatal accidents, suicides, and murders around the time of the Warren Commission, Jim Garrison's investigation, and the House Select Committee on Assassinations. Some conspiriologists have listed mysterious deaths for more than 100 witnesses. Researchers with a narrower interpretation of "mysterious" come up with around 25 names.

One name appearing in both types of list is Lee Bowers, who saw the assassination from a high tower over looking Dealey Plaza. He gave evidence to the Warren Commission about three cars behind the grassy knoll before the killing and two strangers he saw in the area. He also later explained how he had seen a flash of light from the same area just before the shooting. After giving evidence, Bowers complained of receiving warnings to keep silent. On August 9, 1966, he was killed when his car left an empty road and smashed into a concrete bridge.

Journalists Jim Koethe and Bill Hunter searched Jack Ruby's apartment on the night that he shot Oswald. Hunter was shot dead in 1964 by Officer Creighton Wiggins in a police pressroom. Wiggins claimed to have shot him by accident when he dropped his gun. Jim Koethe was writing a book on the assassination in 1965 when someone broke into his home and killed him with a karate chop to the throat. No one was ever caught for the crime.

BELOW LEFT Winston Scott was the CIA officer in charge of Mexico, with important things to say about his suspicions about Lee Harvey Oswald. However, after his death, the CIA ensured his views did not reach the public.

BELOW RIGHT A convenient accident? William C. Sullivan was a former FBI assistant director. He died in a hunting accident just weeks before he was due to give evidence on JFK's murder to the House Select Committee on Assassinations.

Winston Scott was the CIA officer in charge of Mexico during the period Oswald was alleged to have visited. When Scott retired, he wrote a memoir dealing with the assassination. On April 26, 1971, five days before he was to discuss his manuscript with CIA Director Richard Helms, Scott died of a heart attack. The CIA chief of counterintelligence James Jesus Angleton came and took all Scott's papers away. When his family got the manuscript back, 160 pages were missing.

William C. Sullivan was an FBI assistant director when Kennedy was assassinated. Although a report he wrote became part of the Warren Commission, he privately doubted Oswald's guilt. In 1977, just weeks before he was due to give evidence to the House Select Committee on Assassinations, he was accidentally shot dead by a hunter. Sullivan was just one of six senior FBI officials scheduled to appear before the committee who died within six months of each other.

A more controversial name appearing on some lists is Dorothy Hunt, wife of Watergate conspirator and former CIA officer E. Howard Hunt who confessed on his deathbed to being part of a conspiracy to kill JFK. Dorothy Hunt died when United Airlines Flight 553 crashed on the runway of Chicago Midway International Airport on December 8, 1972. More than $10,500 in cash was found in her purse. On White House tapes, President Nixon is worried about Hunt blowing the "whole Bay of Pigs thing"—his code for JFK's assassination—which would be "very unfortunate both for the CIA and for the country." Nixon aide Chuck Colson told *Time* magazine: "I think they [the CIA] killed Dorothy Hunt."

George de Mohrenschildt was the White Russian oilman linked to the CIA and the unlikely friend of Lee Harvey Oswald. He was also a friend of the future president George H.W. Bush, a fellow oilman who was Director of the CIA in 1976–77. In the months before his death, de Mohrenschildt

THE MAUSER MYSTERY

When Deputy Sheriff Eugene Boone first discovered a gun at the Texas School Book Depository, he and fellow officers Seymour Weitzman and Roger Craig thought it was a 7.65mm Mauser rifle. So did Captain Fritz of Homicide. However, it was soon announced that the rifle with Oswald's print on it was a 6.5mm Mannlicher-Carcano, the type of gun owned by Oswald. All except Roger Craig changed their stories. Craig had seen "Mauser" on the gun barrel and had seen Oswald leave the scene in a car—two things the official version denied.

Craig was fired for discussing evidence with a journalist. He testified at Clay Shaw's trial and, a few weeks after his testimony, someone shot at him as he was walking to his car. In 1973, someone forced his car off the road, and then in 1974 he survived another shooting. In May 1975, Craig was found dead of what were officially declared to be "self-inflicted gunshots."

ABOVE The 6.5mm Mannlicher-Carcano rifle allegedly used in the Kennedy assassination. However, why did some police officers at the time think they saw Mauser stamped on the barrel?

LEFT Firefighters deal with the deadly aftermath of the crash of Flight 553. Surely the CIA would not have crashed an entire plane to dispose of a witness? Nixon's aide Chuck Colson believed they had.

BELOW An enigma to the end. George de Mohrenschildt is alleged to have killed himself just hours after being called by an HSCA investigator. Another "crucial witness" whose death meant he avoided questioning.

had written to Bush complaining of FBI persecution because he was writing a book called *I Am a Patsy! I Am a Patsy!*

On the morning of March 29, 1977, de Mohrenschildt gave an interview to journalist Edward Epstein claiming that his friendship with Oswald was sanctioned by CIA agent J. Walton Moore. In the afternoon, de Mohrenschildt got a card from a Select Committee on Assassinations investigator asking him to get in touch so that he could be questioned by the HSCA. Later in the afternoon, he was found dead by the police. They believed he had committed suicide by placing a shotgun in his mouth and firing it. On hearing of the death, Select Committee chair Richardson Preyer said "He was a crucial witness."

George de Mohrenschildt's death was not the only one on March 29, 1977 that robbed the House Select Committee on Assassinations of a witness. Charles Nicoletti, an assassin for the Chicago Mafia and favored triggerman of mob boss Sam Giancana, was due to give evidence to the Committee. However on March 29, someone shot him three times in the back of a head with a .38 revolver as he sat in his Oldsmobile in a suburban car park. Was his body another marker on the trail of death?

The House Select Committee on Assassinations

In 1975, the American public did not know that, on secret tapes, disgraced former President Richard Nixon had described the Warren Commission as "the greatest hoax that has ever been perpetuated…" However, if they had known, an awful lot of them would have agreed with him. Public trust in government had been corroded by Watergate, Vietnam, and revelations of FBI and CIA activity against it own citizens.

Even more corrosive to public trust had been the work of other "lone assassins." The highly suspect killings of Martin Luther King Jr. and Robert F. Kennedy in 1968 had created a sense that any radical politician was a target for assassination. The slaying of JFK was now placed in the context of a trinity of inspirational leaders stolen from the American public in suspicious murders.

In this febrile atmosphere, the Zapruder film premiered on television, causing a storm of protest and renewing doubt about Kennedy's killing. A poll showed that 87 percent of the American population did not believe that Oswald had acted alone. Congressman Thomas Downing was pushing for a JFK investigation while black politicians were pushing for an official investigation of MLK's death. In 1976, Congress voted to create the 12-member United States House of Representatives Select Committee on Assassinations (HSCA) with Downing as chairman.

Downing appointed Richard Sprague, an attorney with a record of 69 homicide convictions out of 70 prosecutions, as chief counsel to the Committee. Sprague brought together a staff of 170 lawyers and researchers, demanding a budget of $6.5 million for the investigation. Even to cynical conspiriologists, Sprague clearly meant business. Hopes were high that the murder of JFK would be opened to full scrutiny and the

division that a suspected conspiracy over the murder of MLK had caused would be healed.

Martin Luther King Jr. had been shot on the balcony of the Lorraine Motel, Memphis, on April 4, 1968. The previous night he gave a speech in which he had ironically said: "Some began to talk of threats… But it doesn't matter with me now. Because I've been to the mountaintop… I'm not fearing any man."

King was allegedly assassinated by small-time convict James Earl Ray. MLK's murder led to an explosion of outrage and rioting in more than 100 U.S. cities. Yet after the crime, Ray obtained four Canadian passports and fled to England. When he was finally returned to the U.S., he pleaded guilty to avoid the death penalty and was sentenced to 99 years imprisonment. He recanted his confession three days later, claiming he had been framed by a conspiracy. Many close to King, such as campaigner James Lawson, believed MLK was slain by "someone trained or hired by the FBI and acting under orders from J. Edgar Hoover." Allegations

ABOVE Death in Memphis. The dead body of Dr. Martin Luther King lies crumpled on the balcony of the Lorraine Motel in Memphis as his supporters and fellow civil rights activists point in the direction they believed the shot has come from.

emerged that Hoover had met Texas oil billionaire H.L. Hunt—also linked by many to JFK's assassination—to discuss a solution to the King problem.

However, the hopes of conspiriologists were soon dashed. A campaign of smears was unleashed at Sprague. Downing was replaced as chairman and moves made to dismiss Sprague, who eventually resigned when he refused to bow to CIA demands. It was clear the HSCA was not going to be allowed to ask the questions and provide the scrutiny Downing and Sprague had wanted.

Interesting evidence was discovered despite a lack of resources, but the HSCA suffered from conducting its investigation in secret. Many of its own investigators felt the secrecy of the HSCA investigation would mean less scrutiny for any misleading testimony they were given. One new lead was a possible note from Oswald to someone called Mr. Hunt asking for "information concerning my position…before any steps are taken…." Dated November 8, 1963, if genuine it may have linked Oswald to CIA man E. Howard Hunt and oilman H.L Hunt.

Several key witnesses due to be called by the HSCA died before they could give evidence. Amongst these was William C. Sullivan, former Deputy Director of the FBI. In his posthumously published biography Sullivan revealed: "I doubt if he [James Earl Ray] acted alone."

When the HSCA finally reported in 1979, it concluded that Ray had shot MLK and that there was a "likelihood of a conspiracy," but not one involving any U.S. government agency. To many this was a travesty of justice, but to be expected. However, the findings on JFK's assassination were more startling.

The HSCA concluded that Oswald had killed Kennedy. However, on the basis of acoustic evidence recorded by a police motorcycle, it also reported there had been four shots—one of which had been fired from the grassy knoll—and two shooters. Although the HSCA disavowed any idea of involvement by U.S. government agencies, anti-Castro Cuban groups, or the Soviet or Cuban governments in the murder, its report made it official that with two shooters there had to have been a conspiracy—a conspiracy or the wild improbability that two lone gunmen independently decided to kill the President at the same time.

ABOVE LEFT Killer of dreams? Although James Earl Ray was convicted of the assassination of Dr. Martin Luther King, the King family and many others came to believe he was not guilty and that there had been a conspiracy to murder one of America's greatest advocates for justice.

ABOVE Crowds overturn a detective's vehicle in Louisville, Kentucky as a dark storm of anger over the murder of Dr. Martin Luther King rolled across America, leading to riots in more than a 100 U.S. cities.

BELOW Hope dashed on the rocks of reality. A meeting of the House Select Committee on Assassinations tries to find the truth about the murders of King and Kennedy. Conspiracy theorists' high hopes for the HSCA were soon shattered by the inadequate efforts it was able to make.

GAETON FONZI, THE HSCA'S OFFICIAL CONSPIRACY THEORIST

Among the staff of the HSCA investigation was journalist Gaeton Fonzi. Even before investigating the assassination in an official capacity, he had written an article that said: "The Warren Report is a deliberate lie. The Commission's own evidence proves there was a conspiracy to murder President Kennedy." Initially, Fonzi held high hopes for the HSCA, but rapidly became disillusioned. He wrote: "There is not one investigator—not one—who served on the Kennedy task force of the HSCA who honestly feels he took part in an adequate effort, let alone the full and complete investigation mandated by Congress." Fonzi went on to produce one of the best books on the assassination, *The Last Investigation*. However, like everyone else, he will have to wait until 2017 for all the HSCA evidence that remains sealed to be revealed.

Suspect Evidence and Suspect Suspects

To solve any murder mystery, a detective needs two things—evidence and suspects. In the extraordinarily complex murder of JFK, solving anything is hampered by two major problems: suspect evidence and suspect suspects.

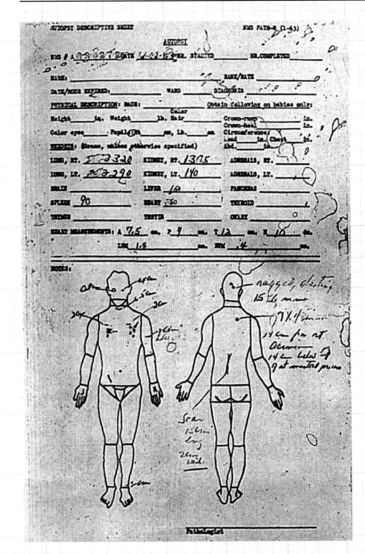

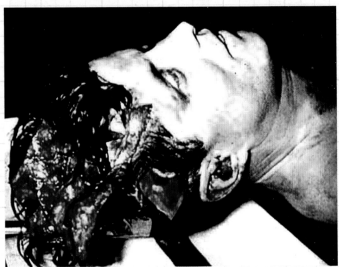

LEFT Diagram of lies? The description sheet for Kennedy's autopsy carried out by Doctor Thorton J. Boswell at Bethesda Naval Hospital. However, it does not match the drawings made at the first autopsy at Parkland Hospital. Today, even the official position is that someone has tampered with the medical evidence.

BELOW The President's brain is missing. This autopsy shot showing the massive damage to John Kennedy's head cannot be squared with other photos showing the same parts of the skull relatively free of damage. Something is seriously wrong with the autopsy photos—either some have been fabricated or they show two different heads.

Huge swathes of vital evidence are missing or were deliberately destroyed. Worse, much of the remaining evidence is suspect, hard to trust as it shows signs of being tampered with. One thing the assassination case is not short of is suspects. However, close examination of the reasons why they are nominated as conspirators usually demonstrates numerous flaws in the theories.

Possibly the most suspect evidence are the autopsy photographs. Doctors who saw Kennedy at Parkland Memorial Hospital testify to his brains having been blown out of a massive hole in the back of his head. The autopsy report carried out under military supervision at Bethesda Naval Hospital in Maryland details a different wound, consistent with being shot from behind. The photographs which appear to show Kennedy's right

temple intact and the back of his head a leaking mess, cannot be squared with photographs showing the back of his head intact and his right temple marred with a huge hole. Either one of the pictures is fabricated or they are of two different heads. Even the autopsy photographer John Stringer testified that he did not take the photographs.

One bit of evidence that could conclusively prove whether Kennedy was shot in the head from the back or from the front would be his brain. However, the brain is missing. Some claim this is because it was given to Robert F. Kennedy to allow for burial, but other official reports show it being examined after JFK's funeral and disappearing in 1965. According to Douglas P. Horne, the Assassination Record Review Boards's chief analyst for military records, there is "unequivocal evidence there was a government cover-up of the medical evidence."

One of the most striking bits of suspect evidence is the Warren Commission's CE399, also known as the "pristine bullet." CE399 was a bullet found on a stretcher at Parkland Memorial Hospital. Despite allegedly being the magic or single bullet that caused all of JFK's and Governor Connally's wounds, it was practically undamaged and free from blood or tissue. The minimal amount of lead missing from the bullet does not appear to correlate with the fragments left in JFK and Connally.

ABOVE March of the assassins? The image of three tramps being marched into custody after the assassination has become a black mirror for conspiriologists, reflecting back their own suspicions. Some see the killers of the President, others see three hoboes.

RIGHT True confession? Convicted killer Charles Harrelson admitted to being one of the "three tramps" and one of the gunmen who killed Kennedy. Can his confession be believed or was it a just a clever con by a convict?

If the physical evidence is tricky, it's nothing to the raft of proposed suspects involved in a conspiracy to kill Kennedy. Among the long list of those who have voluntarily made themselves suspects by confessing to being part of a plot are the names Marita Lorenz, Tex Brown, and James Files. Others such as Roscoe White of the Dallas Police force were put forward by their family. Close examination of any of them throws up enough doubt for many researchers to disregard them totally as suspects.

Photographs of three men, apparently tramps taken into custody on November 22, were seized upon by researchers as showing possible suspects. Several people have been allegedly identified as one of the tramps, including adventurer, artist, and Mafia associate Chauncey Holt; Frank Sturgis, a Watergate burglar and anti-Castro veteran; seismologist and alleged CIA agent Charles Rogers; and Fred Crisman, a man linked to UFOs and 1940s sci-fi stories. The situation was so open that CIA man and Watergate conspirator E. Howard Hunt even lost a libel case in 1985 when he sued a magazine over its claims that he was one of the tramps.

Noted JFK conspiracy author L. Fletcher Prouty—who had served under Kennedy as Chief of Special Operations for the Joint Chiefs of Staff—saw the pictures of the three tramps and noticed a figure in the background that he thought was his old colleague Major General Edward Lansdale, on the basis of his stoop and class ring. Lansdale worked for the Department of Defense on activities such as the anti-Castro Operation Mongoose. Prouty claimed he may have been giving the three men a signal.

However, in 1989, researcher Mary LaFontaine found Dallas Police arrest records for the three tramps—Harold Doyle, John Forrester Gedney, and Gus W. Abrams. Two of the men were still living and confirmed to the FBI that they had been in Dallas on the day of the shooting. This seemed to make a nonsense of the claims that the hoboes were the suspects.

Despite this, many conspiracy researchers refuse to believe that the named vagrants are the men in the photos. They follow the view that an FBI agent once shared with me: "If the Dallas police said my pants were on fire and I could see flames…I'd still not trust them to be telling the truth." In the run-up to his death in 2007, E. Howard Hunt further confused things by claiming that both he and Frank Sturgis were involved in JFK's murder. A study of those suspected may tell us only one thing for sure. In the black mirror of JFK's assassination, we usually see the suspects we expect to see.

CHARLES HARRELSON— TRAMP OR TELLER OF TALL TALES?

It might be hard for most people to comprehend, but many individuals have confessed to being either Kennedy's killer or directly involved in a plot to kill him. One of the most notorious confessors to the crime-of-the-century was Charles Harrelson, the estranged father of Hollywood actor Woody Harrelson. While imprisoned for the assassination of U.S. District Judge John H. Wood, Jr. in a Texas parking lot, Charles Harrelson confessed to being one of the three tramps and one of the gunmen who killed Kennedy. He later withdrew his confession. However, Mafia associate Chauncey Holt also confessed to being one of the tramps. Though he claimed his role in the assassination plot was providing fake Secret Service I.D., he maintained that he had been in Dallas with Harrelson. The confessions of Holt and Harrelson are still believed by some conspiriologists.

LEFT General Y. Major General Edward Lansdale was the basis for character General Y in Oliver Stone's JFK. It was partly because of what he thought he saw in the background of the questionable three tramps photograph that Colonel Fletcher Prouty accused Lansdale of being in Dallas on November 22.

The Mafia Conspiracy Theory

In 1979, the House Select Committee on Assassinations (HSCA) became the first and only official investigation of JFK's murder to conclude that the assassination was probably the result of a conspiracy. It stated: "President John F. Kennedy was probably assassinated as a result of a conspiracy. The committee is unable to identify the other gunman or the extent of the conspiracy."

The HSCA recommended that the Justice Department continue investigating the assassination. The Justice Department did not pursue it. This is not surprising as the HSCA did not identify the conspirators, only suggesting they may have been individual members of the Mafia, possibly working with individual anti-Castro Cubans.

A Mafia conspiracy to kill Kennedy was not a new idea. Ever since Jack Ruby conveniently ended Oswald's life, the involvement of a minor Mob associate had been seen by some to signify the hidden hand of organized crime. Alongside Ruby, the Mafia conspiracy theory had something else going for it: believable motives.

Joe Kennedy had used his influence with Chicago Mob boss Sam Giancana to secure union support for his son JFK in the crucial West Virginia Primary. Joe also persuaded Giancana to help in the Texas and Chicago vote frauds that won JFK the 1960 presidential election. Unfortunately for the Mafia, before JFK was sworn in as the 35th

President of the United States, Joe suffered a major stroke and no longer had the ability to ensure his son honored any deals with the Mob.

JFK appointed his brother Robert F. Kennedy as Attorney General. RFK had made a name for himself as Chief Counsel to the Senate's anti-Mafia McClellan Committee where he had humiliated Mob bosses Santos Trafficante and Carlos Marcello. In his new position, RFK waged an unprecedented war upon the Mafia and its minions such as union boss

JUDITH EXNER– MAFIA BOSS MISTRESS AND JFK'S LOVER

In February 1960, Frank Sinatra introduced JFK to Judith Campbell (also known as Judith Exner.) The two became lovers. However, this meant that JFK was now part of a bizarre triangle involving himself, Judith, and Chicago Mafia boss Sam Giancana. There is no reason to disbelieve Judith's claims about being the mistress of both men. Her travel documents and appointment book from the time provide good evidence, tying in with other sources such as the official log of White House visitors. However, more controversial were Judith's claims to have been used by Kennedy and Giancana to pass messages to each other over topics such as plots to kill Castro. Details of this were first hinted at in 1975, when Judith was subpoenaed to testify before the Church Committee.

OPPOSITE A friend of yours. JFK and Frank Sinatra talk at a formal banquet. The two became close friends during the 1960 election campaign, when Sinatra sang the theme song for Kennedy—"High Hopes." Bobby Kennedy eventually banned Sinatra from seeing JFK owing to the singer's links to the Mafia.

OPPOSITE BELOW Bizarre love triangle. Judith Exner poses with her first husband, actor William Campbell (right,) and actor Perry Lopez at a film premiere. As the lover of not only JFK but also Mob boss Sam Giancana, Judith became the nexus between the Mafia and the White House.

Jimmy Hoffa. His determination to tackle their power even brought him into conflict with head of the FBI, J. Edgar Hoover, who had once told Congress: "There is no such coalition known as the Mafia."

To begin with, his brother's anti-Mafia crusade did not stop JFK allowing the CIA to work with Mafia bosses Santos Trafficante and Sam Giancana on plans to kill mutual enemy Fidel Castro. It also did not stop JFK enjoying the company of Hollywood singer and Mafia associate Frank Sinatra. Actor Peter Lawford had married into the Kennedy clan and was also part of Sinatra's "Rat Pack." This allowed Sinatra access to the President. It was access the Mob tried to exploit, until RFK banned Sinatra from both the White House and all Kennedy family gatherings.

The Mob hated JFK for the change in his policy over Cuba following the Bay of Pigs Invasion and the Cuban Missile Crisis. They hated what they saw as his breaking of a deal they had made by helping him to get elected. And they hated him for the pain his brother was causing them.

Following the assassination, credible reports were made to the FBI that Carlos Marcello had threatened to take care of Bobby Kennedy by killing JFK. The FBI did not follow up these reports. Santos Trafficante was also alleged to have told an associate before the murder: "Kennedy is in trouble. He will get what is coming to him. Kennedy's not going to make it to the election. He is going to be hit."

Not only did the Mafia have a motive to kill JFK, they had access to the best-organized criminal assassins across the globe. Thanks to their work with the CIA, they also had links with anti-Castro Cubans trained in assassination. And they had men on the ground in Texas. In the days before Kennedy's murder, Jack Ruby contacted both Trafficante and Marcello. Influential mobster John Roselli, a key figure in Sam Giancana's Chicago syndicate, had been flown from New Orleans to Garland, Texas, on November 21. Roselli along with Giancana had worked with the Warren Commission member and former head of the CIA Allen Dulles on a plan to kill Castro.

After the assassination, the FBI concluded Marcello was "not a significant figure in organized crime," earning his living as "a tomato salesman." On this basis, the Warren Commission concluded that the link between him and Ruby was insignificant. In 1976, Senator Frank Church's Select Committee to Study Governmental Operations with Respect to Intelligence Activities wanted to recall Roselli to question him about JFK's assassination. Shortly afterward, Roselli disappeared. His body was eventually discovered in a steel drum floating off Miami. Strangely, Sam Giancana was also murdered before he could appear before Church's Committee.

However, many conspiriologists dismiss the Mafia theory on the basis that whilst the Mob might have been able to kill Kennedy, it would not have the ability to hide the conspiracy. It is one thing to kill a president, it is another to destroy evidence and ensure a cover-up in the highest echelons of power.

ABOVE American gangster. Chicago Mafia boss Sam Giancana was murdered shortly before he was due to testify to the Church Committee regarding Mob links with the CIA and his possible involvement in the Kennedy assassination. Was he killed by the Mafia for defiling *omertà*—its code of silence—or by the CIA who feared he would reveal too much?

RIGHT Sealing his fate? JFK signing the three anti-racketeering bills requested by his brother, Attorney General Robert Kennedy, to give the government additional weapons to fight the Mafia. Watched by RFK, J. Edgar Hoover, and others, was this the moment JFK signed his own death warrant by betraying the Mafia who had helped elect him?

The Cuban Conspiracy Theory

When the House Select Committee on Assassinations reported that President John F. Kennedy was probably murdered as the result of a conspiracy, they did not ascribe any organization as being behind it. However, they did make some hints as to the identity of the conspirators, stating that they were possibly individual Mafia members, and potentially working alongside individual members of "anti-Castro Cuban groups."

On the basis of evidence that the Committee had heard, a Mafia and anti-Castro Cuban conspiracy was far from a wild theory. The HSCA had taken credible testimony on the hatred for JFK held by elements of the anti-Castro Cuban exile community and of its links with the Mafia and CIA. It had also taken the testimony of William Robert Plumlee, a pilot and covert operative for the CIA.

Prior to the overthrow of Cuban President Fulgencio Batista in 1959, Plumlee had covertly flown arms to the rebels. After Castro took control, he flew weapons to his opponents. Plumlee worked as part of Operation 40, a CIA-sponsored group of agents dedicated to overthrowing Castro. He had seen the Mafia and anti-Castro Cubans work together on plans to assassinate Castro. Plumlee testified that the day before JFK's murder he had flown key Mafia man Johnny Roselli and two Cubans from Florida to New Orleans and then to Garland, just northeast of Dallas. He believed the men were on a mission to "abort the assassination of President Kennedy."

If Plumlee was telling the truth, the inference was clear. If the Mafia and anti-Castro Cubans knew about the assassination and tried to abort it, then it was likely a Mafia and anti-Castro Cuban conspiracy. However, Plumlee's story was not the oddest tale of Cuban exiles' involvement in a conspiracy to kill Kennedy related to the HSCA.

When Marita Lorenz appeared before the Committee, she not only claimed to be Fidel Castro's former lover, but also witness to a plot by former Operation 40 members Frank Sturgis, Pedro Diaz Lanz, and Orlando Bosch to assassinate Kennedy in Dallas. She also claimed the CIA's E. Howard Hunt and Lee Harvey Oswald were involved. The HSCA

OPERATION 40 BATHED IN BLOOD

Even in the murky world of black operations and contract killing for the CIA, the members of Operation 40 present a remarkable roll call of brutal infamy. Although they never managed to kill Castro, Operation 40 personnel were not untainted with blood. Félix Ismael Rodríguez was involved in the summary execution of Che Guevara; Luis Clemente Faustino Posada Carriles is wanted for the murder of 78 people in the bombing of Cubana Flight 455 in 1976; and Orlando Bosch founded the Coordination of United Revolutionary Organizations—labeled by the FBI as an anti-Castro terrorist umbrella organization—that murdered former Chilean minister Orlando Letelier. Before his murder in 1986, Operation 40 member and drug smuggler Barry Seal told an associate: "You know what they used to call us in Operation 40? *Los bastardos.* The Bastard Squad."

dismissed her account as unreliable. However, Lorenz's tale contained three elements featuring in many conspiracy theories promoting anti-Castro Cubans as the assassins of JFK: a motive dating back to the Bay of Pigs, links to Operation 40, and Frank Sturgis.

When JFK followed Allen Dulles's advice to authorize a CIA-backed invasion of Cuba in January 1961, he had no comprehension of how it would come to haunt his presidency. Owing in part to Dulles's duplicity, the invasion by the anti-Castro Cuban exile Brigade 2506 turned into the disastrous failure known as the Bay of Pigs. As if the number of Cuban dead was not enough reason for anti-Castro exiles to hate JFK, he later scaled down his support for their covert war following the missile crisis of 1962. This was seen as a betrayal. Their extreme bitterness can be gauged from the number of death threats made against Kennedy from the exile community in Florida and the seriousness the Secret Service placed upon them when the President visited the state.

LEFT Public enemy number one. Cuban leader Fidel Castro became the top target for assassination by a strange collection of mutual interests, ranging from the CIA to the Mafia to Cubans forced into exile by his regime.

RIGHT A parade of defeat. Handcuffed and defeated, soldiers of fortune and Cuban members of Assault Brigade 2506 are held captive after their disastrous defeat at the Bay of Pigs.

Revenge and the belief that a new president would be more favorable to their cause—especially if it was thought that a pro-Castro communist killed JFK—is a plausible murder motive. The extremist Cuban exile underground also had the means to conduct a plot. The covert CIA-backed war against Castro's Cuba led to the creation of Operation Mongoose which provided covert training and weapons for anti-Castro Cubans to use for assassinations. The majority of field agents who had been in the Operation 40 assassination group were Cuban, and were well placed to be recruited into any conspiracy. Operation 40 was also closely tied to key players in the Texas oil industry including George H.W. Bush and Jack Crichton.

One member of Operation 40 who has been consistently linked to JFK's assassination is Frank Sturgis. The future Watergate burglar was of Cuban ancestry. A soldier of fortune, he had originally trained Castro's troops in guerrilla warfare before becoming involved in the fight against him. One of Sturgis's closest comrades in both Operation 40 and Watergate was Cuban-born Bernard Barker. When Barker's photo was shown on TV as a result of the Watergate scandal, a Dallas policeman recognized him as the man he had seen on the grassy knoll claiming to be a Secret Service agent.

A Cuban conspiracy may make sense of Jack Ruby and Lee Harvey Oswald's involvement. Ruby had been involved in running guns to Cuba in the 1950s. Despite publicly backing Castro, Oswald was demonstrably linked to the anti-Castro underground through Operation Mongoose players such as Guy Banister and David Ferrie. Strangely, Oswald had been in Ferrie's Civil Air Patrol as had Operation 40 member Barry Seal.

Would an anti-Castro Cuban conspiracy have the power to organize an effective cover-up? No. However, their allies in the CIA would.

ABOVE Brothers in arms. The picture shows anti-Castro activist David Ferrie (circled on left) and a teenage Lee Harvey Oswald (circled on right) in the Civil Air Patrol run by Ferrie. The Patrol also had Operation 40 operative Barry Seal as a member.

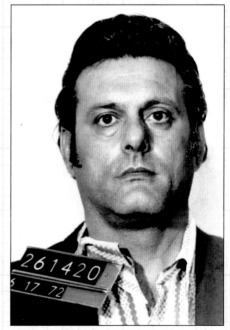

ABOVE The face of an assassin. Mug shot of Frank Sturgis taken at the time of his capture as part of the team who broke into the Democratic National Headquarters sparking the Watergate scandal. Sturgis was a mercenary and assassin who killed dozens of Cubans before being accused by some of being one of JFK's killers.

The CIA Conspiracy Theory

There is so much credible material placing the CIA in any conspiracy to kill Kennedy that it is almost impossible to come up with a theory that does not include them. Within hours of the shooting of JFK in Dealey Plaza, the CIA can be demonstrated to have begun destruction of evidence relating to their knowledge of, and involvement with, Lee Harvey Oswald. Information not destroyed was systematically withheld—not just from the public, but also from the Warren Commission and later the House Select Committee on Assassinations.

I and many other researchers have filed Freedom of Information (F.O.I.) requests to obtain documents the CIA has on the assassination. Former *Washington Post* editor Jefferson Morley initiated an F.O.I. lawsuit against the CIA and discovered they still hold more than a thousand documents they will not release till 2017. They claim we cannot see them owing to reasons of "national security." If Oswald was a simple lone gunman, where is the issue of national security?

Prominent American historians such as David Kaiser and Gerald McKnight have concluded that there was indeed a conspiracy to kill JFK, which included either senior CIA officials or disgruntled operatives. It is said that when Kennedy was assassinated, the British Intelligence service MI6 believed it was a CIA plot. The French secret service organization DGSE went further in 1968, arranging for publication of the book *Farewell America* alleging JFK's murder was arranged by the CIA and Texas oilmen.

JFK was obsessed with spy novels and counted Ian Fleming as a friend. He felt he knew about espionage, but after the Bay of Pigs debacle he said, "How could I have been so stupid to trust the CIA?" According to a CIA report, President Kennedy said he wanted to "splinter the CIA into a thousand pieces and scatter it into the winds." To many conspiracy theorists, this is motive enough for his murder. Kennedy had sacked

Director of the CIA Allen Dulles and his Deputy Director Charles Cabell—whose brother Earle was the Mayor of Dallas and was involved in planning JFK's trip to the city. In 1963, there were a lot of embittered people in American intelligence worried about Kennedy's plans for the CIA and his winding down of the covert war on Cuba.

A large part of the work of the CIA was assassination. Its agents who have been named as possible conspirators, such as David Atlee Phillips, David Sanchez Morales, E. Howard Hunt, and Frank Sturgis, were all well versed in the sort of operation required to kill Kennedy. Public perception of the CIA's role was evident when Hunt sued a magazine for libel over allegations of being involved in the conspiracy and lost, the jury believing evidence that he had been in Dallas on the day.

If there was a CIA conspiracy, it may have been sanctioned by two of the men tasked with investigating the assassination—Allen Dulles and the CIA Director of Counterintelligence James Jesus Angleton. Dulles was a member of the Warren Commission and Angleton the CIA officer in charge of liaison with it. At the CIA, Angleton had run fake defectors into

ABOVE Who watches the watchmen? Before his assassination, JFK had spoken of splintering the CIA into a "thousand pieces and scattering it to the winds." The level of antagonism between him and the Agency was acute and deep-burning.

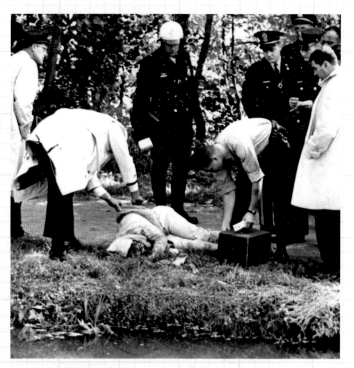

Russia and conducted operations against the Soviet embassy in Mexico. He suppressed information in both areas relating to Oswald.

In 1964, after the murder of renowned Washington artist Mary Pinchot Meyer, her sister Tony was looking for the dead woman's diary when she found Angleton in Mary's studio already searching for it. Mary was the former wife of Cord Meyer—one of the CIA's top men—and also the lover of Timothy Leary and John F. Kennedy. Tony eventually found the diary and, discovering it contained sensitive information, handed it over to Angleton. The CIA claim Angleton destroyed the diary.

While walking beside a canal in Georgetown, Washington, D.C., Mary had been shot twice—once in the back of the head and once in the heart. Despite an extensive search, no murder weapon was ever found and the African-American homeless man charged with the murder was found not guilty. The judge at the trial, Howard Corcoran, had recently been

appointed by President Johnson and prevented disclosure of information about Meyer's private life in court. Just before his death in 2001, Cord Meyer told author C. David Heymann that the people who killed Mary were "the same sons of bitches that killed John F. Kennedy."

In another deathbed confession, in 2007, E. Howard Hunt admitted his own role in the "Big Event." He named CIA men David Phillips, Frank Sturgis, William Harvey, David Sanchez Morales, and Cord Meyer as fellow conspirators alongside Lyndon Johnson.

However, this was not good enough for many conspiracy theorists who believe the CIA was not involved in the killing, only in the cover-up of its bungled running of Lee Harvey Oswald as an agent. For them, an even darker force than the CIA was behind the assassination: the shadowed but all-embracing power of the military-industrial complex.

ALLEN DULLES
ALL-AMERICAN TRAITOR?

With his spectacles and pipe, Allen Dulles looked more like an academic than the man who shaped the modern intelligence system of the United States. A ruthless innovator, it was under Dulles as Director that the CIA mind-control project MK-ULTRA was initiated, as was the U-2 spy-plane program. Dulles's direction of the agency brought about successful pro-American coups in Iran and Guatemala. The coup in Guatemala saved the American multinational United Fruit Company from having its land in the country nationalized. Interestingly, Dulles was on the company's board of trustees. Would his dismissal from the CIA be a motive for killing Kennedy? Was Dulles capable of that sort of treason? Supreme Court Justice Arthur Goldberg thought so, branding Dulles a "traitor" for his covert support of Nazi enterprises during World War II.

The Military-Industrial Complex Conspiracy Theory

President Dwight D. Eisenhower was a five-star general and a World War II hero who had gone from the top of the military establishment to being the most powerful politician in the world. However, as he left office in 1961, Eisenhower did something unheard of—he used his last presidential address to the nation to warn it of the dangers of something he labeled "the military-industrial complex."

In a speech that has gone down in history, Eisenhower said: "This conjunction of an immense military establishment and a large arms industry is new in the American experience. The total influence—economic, political, even spiritual—is felt in every city, every statehouse, every office of the federal government… we must not fail to comprehend its grave implications…

"In the councils of government, *we must guard against the acquisition of unwarranted influence, whether sought or unsought, by the military-industrial complex*. The potential for the disastrous rise of misplaced power exists and will persist.

"We must never let the weight of this combination endanger our liberties or democratic processes. We should take nothing for granted."

In the years since JFK's assassination, the most persistent conspiracy theory has become that the shadowy forces of the military-industrial complex had him killed. The claim is that this was done as part of a military coup d'état by the Joint Chiefs of Staff (JCS)—including its chairman General Maxwell D. Taylor—in combination with the military intelligence and the CIA. Their motivation was to remove Kennedy who they believed was winding down the Cold War. For the military-industrial complex, conflict meant massive sales of hardware and career progression.

Following the missile crisis of 1962, Kennedy had done a secret deal with Khrushchev not to invade Cuba, had signed a nuclear test ban treaty, and was planning a massive reduction in military spending. Possibly worst of

all as far as the military-industrial complex was concerned, JFK signed National Security Action Memorandum No. 263 on October 11, 1963, resolving to withdraw all American forces from Vietnam by 1965. No invasion of Cuba, no war in the Far East, and massive military cuts would have cost the military-industrial complex billions of dollars.

The extreme lengths to which the military-industrial complex would go to advance conflict are demonstrated by Operation Northwoods. Developed by military planners during 1962–63, Northwoods proposed that the CIA conduct terrorist hijackings and bombings on U.S. soil that would be falsely flagged as Cuban attacks. Although the JCS approved the plan, President Kennedy personally vetoed it. Strangely, shooting the President and blaming it on Oswald—who could be portrayed as a Cuban sympathizer—sounds like an action typical of Operation Northwoods.

The top echelons of the U.S. military had both the means to carry out the assassination and its subsequent cover-up. They had the best marksmen in the army at their disposal, they could order the 112th Military Intelligence Group to stand down presidential security support, and they could control the autopsy on JFK carried out at Bethesda Naval Hospital.

ABOVE U.S. Secretary of Defense McNamara and U.S. Army Chief-of-Staff General Maxwell Taylor confer with JFK in September 1963 over the latest developments in Vietnam. A few weeks later, Kennedy resolved to withdraw U.S. forces from South-East Asia.

ABOVE The machinery of war. Helicopter manufacturers such as Bell Helicopters were just one section of the military-industrial complex which benefited massively from the billions of dollars spent on the war in Vietnam.

Described by HSCA medical specialist Dr. Cyril Wecht as "one of the most incomplete, superficial, inadequate, inept, forensic pathologically incompetent medical autopsies I have ever seen," the examination of JFK's body was overseen by admirals and generals.

Researcher Stephen M. Birmingham advocated another possible motive for the military-industrial complex wanting to eliminate JFK. He pointed out that ten days before Kennedy's death, the President signed National Security Action Memorandum No. 271, which would have ended the space race against the Soviet Union and led to a possible joint lunar landing program. If enacted, NSAM 271 would have cost the military-industrial complex billions and would have been seen as soft on the Soviets.

Whether or not there was a conspiracy by the military-industrial complex to kill President Kennedy, after his assassination the road to conflict was clear. On November 25, the day of JFK's funeral, President Johnson met with Henry Cabot Lodge, the U.S. ambassador to South Vietnam. The next day, LBJ had signed NSAM 273. This effectively reversed Kennedy's policy of withdrawal and paved the way to America's war against North Vietnam. In December, Johnson told the Joint Chiefs of Staff: "Just let me get elected, and then you can have your war."

The war cost America $173 billion and more than 58,000 dead Americans, while more than 75,000 veterans were left disabled. It cost the lives of at least 2 million Vietnamese. Kennedy's death had ushered in a dark period. With conflict abroad came vast conflict at home. A whole generation was caught up in the divisions caused by the war.

If there was a military-industrial complex conspiracy, it needed not only JFK's death, but also LBJ's agreement to war. Did it have reasons for thinking this would happen? That Johnson could be controled? As many conspiriologists proclaim, the man who became President after the assassination had his own reasons for wanting Kennedy dead.

EISENHOWER, U-2, AND LEE HARVEY OSWALD

Conspirologists such as L. Fletcher Prouty and academics including James Nathan advance the same idea to explain Eisenhower's attack on the military-industrial complex. Both highlight the downing of a CIA U-2 spy plane and the capture of its pilot Gary Powers while on a mission over the Soviet Union in May 1960. The embarrassing incident derailed Eisenhower's planned talks with the Soviets, leading to suspicion that the CIA planned the mission failure. Senator J. William Fulbright said: "I often wondered why, in the midst of efforts by Eisenhower and Khrushchev to come to some understanding, the U-2 incident was allowed to take place. No one will ever know whether it was accidental or not." Gary Powers himself stated that Oswald's defection to the Soviet Union with U-2 secrets may have had a bearing on his being shot down.

ABOVE Unlikely prophet of doom. Former top general President Dwight D. Eisenhower used his televised farewell speech to warn the American people about the dangers posed by the military-industrial complex.

BELOW *Hey, Hey, LBJ, How Many Kids Did You Kill Today?* The Vietnam war tore American society apart, as students and other protestors clashed daily with the forces of state authority.

The LBJ Conspiracy Theory

Lyndon Baines Johnson was miserable as Vice President of the United States. The vast political influence he had wielded as Senate majority leader had evaporated. Instead of being President Kennedy's trusted lieutenant, he was overshadowed by Attorney General Bobby Kennedy. The two men hated each other. LBJ had to suffer knowing that Bobby's aides regularly passed around a toy voodoo doll of him.

In 1963, Johnson felt so depressed that some days he could not get out of bed. His drinking was getting out of control. He knew President Kennedy was preparing to drop him from the Democratic ticket in the coming 1964 presidential election as a result of the possibility of three major scandals about Johnson coming to light.

LBJ's relationship with Texas businessman Billie Sol Estes—who had operated a multi-million fraud against the government—was coming under scrutiny. Just as damaging, LBJ's protégé and Senate official Bobby Baker was being investigated for corrupt practices, Mafia links, and activities at his Quorum Club where Washington politicians obtained sexual services. Author Robert Winter-Berger recorded LBJ as saying: "That son-of-a-bitch [Baker] is going to ruin me. If that c***sucker talks I'm going to land in jail." On the day of the assassination itself, a secret session of the Senate Rules Committee was hearing evidence that LBJ had received a $100,000 payoff for his role in bringing the TFX fighter plane contract to Fort Worth.

On November 22, 1963, barring some miracle, it seemed that LBJ's political career was over and that he was facing prison. The bullet that brutally ended JFK's life benefited many people, but there is no one for whom it was more of a godsend than LBJ. With the full power of the presidency behind him, Johnson was able to quash further investigation into his alleged corruption.

James Wagenvoord, former editorial business manager for *Life* magazine, claims that based on information they received from Robert Kennedy, *Life* were planning an exposé on LBJ and Bobby Baker. The story was dropped. The issue that would have carried it instead featured the Zapruder film.

As researchers such as Barr McClellan have pointed out, a large amount of circumstantial evidence locates LBJ at the heart of a conspiracy to kill Kennedy. LBJ's mistress Madeleine Brown placed him at meeting with future Warren Commission member John McCloy and Texan oil barons Clint Murchinson and H.L. Hunt where Kennedy was discussed. After the meeting, LBJ told Brown: "Kennedy will never embarrass me again."

Strangely, Mafia associate Eugene Brading was arrested for acting suspiciously in the Dal-Tex Building overlooking Dealey Plaza on November 22. The day before, Brading had been in H.L Hunt's office, very possibly with Jack Ruby. At around midnight on November 21, Ruby visited Brading at the Cabana Motel in Dallas. Brading was later arrested and released over the assassination of RFK.

In 1998, researcher Walt Brown revealed that the only previously unidentified fingerprint found at the "snipers' nest" at the Texas School Book Depository had been identified as belonging to Malcolm "Mac" Wallace. The fingerprint was probably left on the day of the assassination. Mac Wallace was a close associate of LBJ. In 1951, he had been found guilty of murdering John Kinser, the lover of LBJ's sister Josefa. Despite 11 members of the jury at his trial wanting him to get the death penalty,

Wallace got a suspended sentence. His bail and legal team were arranged by LBJ.

In prison, Jack Ruby urged researchers to read the book *A Texan Looks at Lyndon* by J. Evetts Haley, which exposed LBJ's corrupt relationship with Billie Sol Estes. Ruby suggested it was central to the JFK conspiracy. In 1984, Billie Sol Estes, who had served prison time for his massive fraud, instructed his lawyer to write to the Justice Department. In the letter he claimed to have knowledge that LBJ had used Wallace to kill nine people, including JFK. The Justice Department did not investigate further.

LBJ arranged JFK's trip to Dallas. With support from fellow members of the Suite 8F Group and oilmen like Hunt, he could easily have arranged a conspiracy in Texas to kill the President. However, could LBJ have arranged the following cover-up?

Yes. Beyond appointing the Warren Commission members, the power of the presidency gave him the ability. LBJ could also have benefited from his close relationship with J. Edgar Hoover. The two men walked their dogs together for 19 years. It is demonstrable that the FBI removed, created, and edited evidence relating to the assassination. Was this done on Hoover's orders to help his friend LBJ?

In 2011, suggestions emerged that Jackie Kennedy believed that LBJ and a cabal of southern businessmen were behind her husband's murder. Material on her views is sealed at the Kennedy Library until 2067. However, within a week of JFK's death, Jackie and Bobby Kennedy sent a message to Moscow officials stating that they believed that "the President was felled by domestic opponents."

SUITE 8F GROUP
THE MEN WHO RULED TEXAS

The paranoid nightmare of many conspiracy theorists, a smoke-filled room populated by top businessmen and politicians secretly shaping the world, is just sometimes conspiracy fact. Suite 8F of the Lamar Hotel in Houston, Texas gave its name to a group of the most powerful southern businessmen and politicians who met there regularly to advance a right-wing agenda, and their own careers and causes. Amongst its members were LBJ, John Connally, George and Herman Brown of military contractor Brown & Root, and multi-millionaire Jesse H. Jones. Suite 8F also represented the interests of oil barons Clint Murchison and H.L. Hunt, Bell Helicopter, Billie Sol Estes, and Bobby Baker. When LBJ resigned as President, Richard Nixon was co-opted into the group. Some conspiriologists contend that any JFK conspiracy must have its origins in the secret dealings of Suite 8F.

ABOVE Spider at the heart of the web. Oil baron Clint Murchison Sr. was an old friend of FBI director J. Edgar Hoover and a central member of the shadowy group that met at Suite 8F. Allegations have been made that he hosted at least one meeting at his home where murdering President Kennedy was discussed.

BELOW Bad news. President Lyndon B. Johnson calls the Kennedy family after learning of Senator Robert Kennedy's assassination in June 1968. However, some in the Kennedy family believed LBJ was responsible for arranging the assassination of JFK.

JFK the Film

To many film critics, the silver screen is a reflective mirror—Hollywood telling stories that replicate the aspirations, emotions, and concerns of America. To others, Hollywood is hokum, a way of selling overpriced popcorn. However, there is no denying that some films carve out a place in the cultural landscape, giving them real import and allowing them to influence the world they seek to reflect.

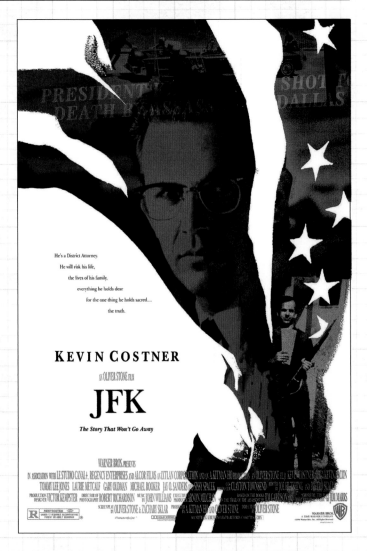

Written, produced, and directed by Oliver Stone, *JFK* (1991) became a movie that mattered. Instead of just telling a story about the investigation of the assassination of John F. Kennedy, it ended up becoming a part of it. However, before getting to that point, it faced unprecedented levels of criticism from critics and from key elements of Hollywood itself.

Before embarking on the JFK project, Oliver Stone was best known for his Oscar-winning films on the Vietnam War—*Platoon* (1986) and *Born on the Fourth of July* (1989.) According to Stone, he was attracted to making JFK because "The murder of President Kennedy was a seminal event for me and millions of Americans. It changed the course of history. It was a crushing blow to our country and to millions of people around the world. It put an abrupt end to a period of innocence and idealism."

Stone wrote the *JFK* script with Zachary Sklar, a journalism professor who had helped Jim Garrison with the manuscript of his 1988 book *On the Trail of the Assassins*. Their script took material from Garrison's book and Jim Marrs' *Crossfire: The Plot That Killed Kennedy* (1989,) turning it into a taut examination of the lead-up to and later cover-up of the conspiracy to kill JFK. The film is centred on Jim Garrison and his 1969 trial of Clay Shaw. Stone called the fictionalized account a "counter-myth" to the "official fictional myth of the Warren Commission."

Whilst the film was still shooting, critical attacks upon it and Stone began. The *Chicago Tribune* ran a story calling the movie "an insult to intelligence". The national security correspondent of *The Washington Post*, George Lardner, managed to get onto the set and acquire a copy of a draft script. In a powerful, contemptuous article entitled *On the Set: Dallas in Wonderland; How Oliver Stone's Version of the Kennedy Assassination Exploits the Edge of Paranoia*, he attacked it for "chasing a fiction." Stone was stung into an official response to Lardner, but the attacks kept coming.

Much of the worst criticism was focused on Stone's suggestion that LBJ was at some level a participant in a coup d'état against JFK. Jack Valenti, president of the influential Motion Picture Association of America, became one of *JFK*'s most virulent critics. Comparing it to Leni Reifenstahl's *Triumph of the Will*, he wrote: "Both *JFK* and *Triumph of the Will* are equally a propaganda masterpiece and equally a hoax. Mr. Stone and Leni Reifenstahl have another genetic linkage: neither of them carried a disclaimer on their film that its contents were mostly pure fiction."

Valenti had been in charge of the press in Dallas on November 22, 1963. Visible in the photograph of LBJ being sworn in, he became the new President's special assistant. In Washington circles, people joked Valenti would spin "LBJ dropping the H-bomb as an urban renewal project."

When the film was finally released in December 1991, some critics such as Pat Dowell resigned when their papers would not print positive reviews. After a slow start at the box office, *JFK* began to garner both praise and strong receipts, earning more than $205 million worldwide.

ABOVE Former aide to LBJ Jack Valenti was President of the Motion Picture Association of America and in the forefront of the Hollywood establishment attacking *JFK*.

ABOVE RIGHT Controversial "counter-myth" or "crock of crap"? Stone labeled his film "a counter-myth to the official myth of the Warren Commission." Some critics were a lot less kind in their descriptions even before the film hit the screen.

The film resonated strongly with American filmgoers. Widespread outrage was caused by the ending of the film, which proclaimed: "The files of the House Select Committee on Assassinations are locked away until the year 2029." Public pressure mounted to the point where President Bush signed the President John F. Kennedy Assassination Records Collection Act of 1992 (also known as the *JFK* Act). This led to the formation of the Assassination Records Review Board, which has released vast amounts of previously classified documents. By law, all existing assassination-related documents will be made public by 2017.

Despite this huge legal legacy, the film is still unpopular with those trying to debunk JFK conspiracy theories. Vincent Bugliosi, best known for prosecuting Charles Manson, attacked it in his 2007 book *Reclaiming History*. He lists 32 "lies and fabrications" and slams *JFK* as "one continuous lie in which Stone could not find any level of deception and invention beyond which he was unwilling to go."

As Stone found out, when it comes to JFK's murder, everyone who holds an opinion is a critic of someone else.

ABOVE Courtroom crusader vs. the conspiracy. Kevin Costner as District Attorney Jim Garrison demonstrating flaws in the Warren Commission version of events in Dealey Plaza.

BELOW Right direction. Kevin Costner getting direction from Oliver Stone on the set of *JFK*.

JFK VS. THE OSCARS

JFK has gone down in Hollywood annals as having opened to a storm of criticism and abuse, both in terms of fury and scale, rarely seen before or since. However, it weathered this outcry, becoming more than just a box office success. The critical tide turned and *JFK* received eight Oscar nominations. Although winning only two, for Best Cinematography and Best Film Editing, Oliver Stone was rewarded for the abuse he suffered over *JFK* with a Golden Globe for Best Director. During his acceptance speech, he said: "A terrible lie was told to us 28 years ago. I hope that this film can be the first step in righting that wrong." Ultimately, the role *JFK* played in creating greater transparency through the Assassinations Records Review Board may be its highest accolade.

The Kennedy Curse

The brutal killings of John F. Kennedy and Robert F. Kennedy were played out on the most public of stages. Millions saw the scarring images of both men slain and witnessed life, love, and hope extinguished in the casual brutality of bullets. The Kennedy clan's grief and mourning had to be shared with a global media and its audience.

We, the public, have never let that sense of tragedy become detached from the family. Each new incident befalling any Kennedy is linked in many minds to an ongoing chain of sorrow. Given the easy label of the "Kennedy curse," there is no escaping that the clan has become synonymous with premature death.

Though the assassinations are seared into the public memory as the instants when tragedy first afflicted the Kennedy family, sadness dogged them long before the shots rang out. Rose Marie "Rosemary" Kennedy was the third child and first daughter of Joseph Kennedy Sr. and his wife Rose. Suffering from learning difficulties, Rosemary lived a sheltered life.

The Winnie-the-Pooh-loving young woman enjoyed a world that her own diary records as filled with tea dances, dress fittings, and family outings. She was even presented to King George VI and Queen Elizabeth. Then in 1941, at the age of 23, her father had her lobotomized. Left incontinent, infantile, and unintelligible, Rosemary spent the rest of her life hidden away in institutions before dying in 2007.

Tragedy struck the family again in 1944 when JFK's elder brother Joseph died on a U.S.A.F. bombing run over the English Channel. A plane crash also took the life of his sister Kathleen Agnes "Kick" Cavendish in 1948. Having married the protestant William Cavendish in 1944 and become the Marchioness of Hartington, "Kick" was ostracized by her family. Only Joseph Kennedy Sr. went to her funeral, her mother having discouraged her siblings from attending.

Just seven months after JFK's assassination, his youngest brother Senator Edward M. Kennedy, better known as "Ted", almost died in a light aircraft crash. Ted Kennedy was pulled from the wreckage by fellow Senator Birch E. Bayh II. With a punctured lung, internal bleeding, broken ribs, and a severely damaged back, he was lucky to survive and spent months in hospital. Despite the best efforts of some conspiracy theorists to prove otherwise, it is almost certain that the crash was caused simply by atrocious weather conditions.

After the murder of his sole remaining brother in 1968, Ted was the Kennedy patriarch, becoming surrogate father to 13 nephews and nieces, and negotiating the marriage contract between Jacqueline Kennedy and Aristotle Onassis. By early 1969, he was front-runner for the Democratic nomination in 1972. Ted was reluctant, stating: "I know I'm going to get my ass shot off one day, and I don't want to."

ABOVE LEFT The Kennedy curse strikes again? The wreck of the light aircraft makes it quite clear how lucky Teddy Kennedy was to survive the 1964 plane crash.

LEFT Wrecked—Senator Edward Kennedy's car with smashed windshield after his accident at Chappaquiddick. The incident claimed the life of Mary Jo Kopechne and wrecked Teddy's chances of becoming president.

Of all the Kennedys, none is more emblematic of the traumas endured by his extended clan than David Anthony Kennedy. Only 11 days before his 13th birthday, David's father Robert F. Kennedy saved him from drowning. Still recovering the next night, David stayed up to watch his father win the California Democratic primary. Elation turned to horror when scenes of RFK's triumph gave way to the horror of his assassination live on TV before his son's eyes. David never recovered from the emotional damage of this moment. Despite wealth, rock star looks, and a talent for journalism, his life was a constant attempt to escape the gravity of drug addiction. In 1984, aged 29, the dead body of David Kennedy was found in a Florida hotel. Medical reports showed he died from an overdose of anti-psychotic medication, opiate-based painkillers and cocaine.

The matter was taken out of his hands by another tragic twist in the Kennedy tale. After a party, during the early hours of July 19, 1969, the Senator drove his car off a bridge linking Chappaquiddick Island to Martha's Vineyard. Kennedy escaped the vehicle, but his passenger—28-year-old Mary Jo Kopechne—drowned. Kennedy did not report the accident for several hours, by which time Kopechne's body had been found. The subsequent inquest found that "aspects of Kennedy's story of that night were not true." The Chappaquiddick incident ruined his reputation and presidential chances.

Many conspiracy theorists are unsatisfied with official accounts of the incident, believing Kennedy was framed. Some point out that Mary Jo Kopechne once lived with Nancy Carole Tyler in Washington. If anyone had the inside track on the Bobby Baker scandal that was helping to convince JFK that he should dump LBJ as Vice President in 1964, it was Tyler as Baker's secretary. Tyler died in a plane crash in 1965.

However, it is another plane crash and episode in the so-called Kennedy curse that most excites some conspiriologists. While the death of Robert's son Michael LeMoyne Kennedy in a 1997 skiing accident aroused little suspicion, the death of John F. Kennedy Jr. is another matter. Within hours of the Piper Saratoga aircraft that he was piloting crashing into the sea off Martha's Vineyard in 1997, the Internet was awash with speculation about both the Kennedy curse and possible sabotage of the plane. However, the official report on the death of John F. Kennedy Jr., his wife Carolyn, and his sister-in-law Lauren Bessette, attributed "pilot error" as the probable cause.

Logically, the Kennedy curse is nonsense. Occultist conspiriologists' theory that it is the result of an actual hex seems risible. However, the curse works as an idea that the public can project their feelings about the family onto. It also works figuratively because it is an unavoidable truth that the Kennedy family have walked at length through the shadow of sorrow.

ABOVE Senator Edward M. Kennedy congratulates his nephew, David Kennedy, upon his graduation. David's whole life seemed blighted with trauma and tragedy after seeing the murder of his father Robert F. Kennedy broadcast live on television.

RIGHT A proud U.S. flag flies on an impromptu memorial to John F. Kennedy Jr. on July 22, 1999 atop the Gay Head cliffs in the town of Aquinnah on the island of Martha's Vineyard, MA. On the horizon, the sailors aboard the USS *Briscoe* bury the remains of JFK Jr., his wife Carolyn Bessette Kennedy, and her sister Lauren Bessette at sea.

The Wilder Shores of Conspiracy AKA the "No Bullet" Territory

Kennedy's killing was, as Bill Hicks said, "the ground zero of conspiracy culture". The huge gaping wound left on the collective American mind has turned the events in Dealey Plaza into a magnet for crazy ideas. In the world of serious research into JFK's murder, the oddest theories are known as "the wilder shores". They are also known as "no bullet territory".

A list of those that supposedly murdered JFK will boggle any mind with both its length and diversity. During the last 20 years as a parapolitics author, I have received communications telling me the JFK conspiracy was organized by: the British royal family; the Freemasons; Mossad; alien shapeshifters; interdimensional shapeshifters; Bobby Kennedy; the Tavistock Institute; the Order of Elect Cohens; the Fourth Reich; and a dozen assorted occult orders.

The "evidence" given by those offering theories from the wilder shores of conspiracy often redefines the meaning of "scant". Masonic involvement is "proved" because Dallas is ten miles north from the 33rd degree of latitude and the 33rd degree is the highest Freemasonry order. While shaking with disbelief at this, consider the idea that JFK was actually shot by a flechette fired from an umbrella. Conspiriologists diverge over whether the umbrella fired a poison dart, paralyzing Kennedy before the fatal head shot, or whether the umbrella delivered the coup de grace itself.

An umbrella deathblow seems almost reasonable compared to other "no bullet" theories such as claims that Kennedy's head exploded through the workings of a powerful psychic or a faulty alien implant. I once saw a theory cause a fistfight, when one conspiriologist announced to another: "Any moron knows ballistics prove Jackie Kennedy shot her husband with a hidden gun." Bizarrely, there are hundreds of websites backing the Jackie-as-killer theory.

However, the most popular of the shooter theories that screams against rationality involves limousine driver and secret service agent William Greer. Despite film and photographic evidence that convinces most people Greer's hands never left the steering wheel, conspiriologist William Cooper saw otherwise. His extensive promotion of Greer as killer on radio shows has made it a cult belief.

Some of the conspiracy flotsam and jetsam washing up from the wilder shores is less dismissible. Those seeing a Nazi connection to Kennedy's death are at least able to produce evidence that key CIA personnel were deeply connected to former Nazi spymaster Reinhard Gehlen, and that Operation Paperclip brought many Nazi scientists to America after World War II. For example, former head of the V-2 rocket program Dr. Walter Robert Dornberger worked for Bell Helicopter in 1963. He was the boss of Michael Paine, and it was Michael Paine and his wife Ruth who gave a home to Marina Oswald and helped Lee Harvey Oswald find work at the T.S.B.D.

ABOVE Was JFK a Mission Control problem? Recently revealed memos from President Kennedy to NASA have made previously wild-sounding claims of a NASA-related motive to the assassination seem somewhat more credible.

LEFT Out of this world theory. Major Jesse Marcel from the Roswell Army Air Field with debris found 75 miles northwest of Roswell, NM, in June 1947. Many UFOlogists have always argued that Kennedy's murder was linked to a cover-up of Roswell and the U.S. military's knowledge of U.F.Os.

Those in the U.F.O. community who were laughed at for years for suggesting JFK's assassination was related to a cover-up of U.F.O. evidence got a boost in 2011. A CIA memo showing that Kennedy wrote to the agency's director just ten days before his death asking to see their U.F.O. files was released owing to a Freedom of Information request. Strangely, the released memo seems to back up a leaked document sent to U.F.O. researcher Timothy Cooper in 1999 talking of JFK making "inquiries regarding our activities, which we cannot allow".

Another released memo also shows that 10 days before the assassination, JFK wrote to NASA to instruct them to work closely with the Soviet Union on space exploration. Researcher Stephen M. Birmingham has always made a convincing argument that JFK was defying the military-industrial complex with National Security Memorandum 271. Signed by Kennedy on November 12, it advocated a U.S.-Soviet lunar landing program. NSM 271 was kept secret for almost 20 years after Kennedy's death.

Marina Oswald has offered many different reasons as to why her husband killed Kennedy. On the one occasion I got to speak to her, the only thing she would say was: "Look at the Federal Reserve." In 1994, she told writer A.J. Weberman: "The answer is the Federal Reserve Bank. It is wrong to blame it on Angleton and the CIA only per se. This is only one finger of the same hand. The people who supply the money are above the CIA." Maybe those who believe that the conspiracy was the result of Kennedy's plans to end the power of the Federal Reserve are not so crazy.

However, the craziest assassination theory comes from a possible conspirator. George de Mohrenschildt, the rabid anti-communist White Russian oilman with links to the CIA and a friend of both George H.W. Bush and the Oswald family, had his own idea about what the real murder motivation was. He always blamed the killing on an argument Lee and Marina had about a washing machine.

RIGHT Striking synchronicities. The two most infamous assassinations in American history—the killings of Abraham Lincoln and JFK—share some uncanny coincidences.

BELOW "Look at the Federal Reserve." At times Marina Oswald has blamed a conspiracy relating to the Federal Reserve, headquartered at the Marriner S. Eccles Federal Reserve Board Building in Washington, D.C.

SHOTS OF SYNCHRONICITY

Revolutionary psychiatrist Carl Jung once defined synchronicity as "meaningful coincidence" and the Kennedy assassination certainly has some coincidences. In 1962, J.J. Marric wrote a detective novel entitled *Gideon's March* about a plot to assassinate Kennedy on a visit to London that echoed many elements of JFK's actual death. More widely known are similarities between the assassinations of Kennedy and Abraham Lincoln. In this popular list are nuggets such as: both were elected President in '60; both were elected to Congress in '46; both were succeeded by southerners called Johnson; and both assassins were killed before being tried. Unfortunately some of the supposed synchronicities are no more than modern legends; Lincoln did not have a secretary called Kennedy who warned him not to go to the theater on the evening he was shot.

Assassination Stories— a Modern Media Mythology

Historic events regularly permeate popular culture as they filter through the collective psyche of those who have lived through them. However, portrayals of JFK's assassination in the worlds of fiction often mark it out as more than just a historical turning point. The wealth and nature of the assassination stories that his death inspired amount to a modern media mythology. Fiction seems to provide a necessary response to the wound and resonant mystery lying at the heart of modern American history.

Many claim that cinema is the art form and medium best reflecting turmoil in America's collective soul. Yet, aside from the groundbreaking documentary *Rush to Judgment* (1967,) it took almost a decade for a movie to be made about the events of November 22, 1963. An unsettling mixture of fiction and fact, *Executive Action* was released in November 1973, a fortnight before the tenth anniversary of the killing.

Executive Action tells the assassination from the conspirators' point of view, with the plot originating in a smoky room filled with oil magnates, politicians, and figures from U.S. intelligence. The film ran into a harsh wall of criticism, much of it organized by former LBJ aide Jack Valenti.

With some theaters refusing to show it and TV stations banning its advertising, the film closed before the anniversary of the assassination and was not seen again in America for another decade.

However, the assassination of JFK combined with the murky conspiracies of Watergate, created a swathe of paranoid cinema releases in the 1970s infused with elements of both events. Conspiracy thrillers such as *The Conversation* (1974) and *Three Days of The Condor* (1975) represent an

BOTTOM LEFT American Paranoia. *The Parallax View* is a prime example of conspiracy theory paranoia running through the heart of American cinema in the 1970s.

BOTTOM RIGHT Bang on Target. The 1973 movie *Executive Action* became the first Hollywood film to directly suggest President Kennedy's killing was a conspiracy, in its view, one linked to oil magnates, U.S. intelligence, and top politicians.

As American as apple pie.

Paramount Pictures Presents
AN ALAN J. PAKULA PRODUCTION
WARREN BEATTY
THE PARALLAX VIEW

Co-starring HUME CRONYN · WILLIAM DANIELS AND PAULA PRENTISS
Director of Photography GORDON WILLIS · Music Scored by MICHAEL SMALL
Executive Producer GABRIEL KATZKA · Screenplay by DAVID GILER and LORENZO SEMPLE, Jr.
Produced and Directed by ALAN J. PAKULA · PANAVISION® TECHNICOLOR® A Paramount Picture

RIGHT His Dark Materials—American writer James Ellroy has used the background to JFK's assassinations to produce an acknowledged classic trilogy of great crime novels.

BOTTOM Jeffrey Dean Morgan as the The Comedian from the hit 2009 movie *The Watchmen*.

America no longer trusting of the government's secret men in the shadows. The possible highpoint of the genre is Alan J. Pakula's 1974 movie *The Parallax View*.

Revolving around a reporter played by Warren Beatty, his investigation of one presidential candidate's murder ultimately results in him becoming the patsy of another political assassination. All parallels with JFK's murder are intentional, especially when a commission announces that the killer acted alone and hopes the verdict will end conspiracy theories.

JFK's murder may be the greatest whodunnit and best route into America's recent shadowy history, but it is the basis for surprisingly little crime fiction. One author who uses it to explore the confused undergrowth of criminal connections to the secret state is James Ellroy. Across his acclaimed *Underworld USA Trilogy*, he reflects on many characters, agencies, and elements involved in the assassination. The second book in the trilogy *The Cold Six Thousand* (2001) begins minutes after the shooting, exploring a conspiracy involving the FBI, the CIA, and the Mafia for the next five years, including further plots to murder Martin Luther King Jr. and Bobby Kennedy.

As the death of JFK is a clear nexus point in history, it has been amply covered in the alternative history genre, notably in the divergent universe of Stephen Baxter's *Voyage* (1996.) The bullets of Dealey Plaza have also inspired more time travel stories than any other single event with more than a hundred films, TV episodes, and stories based around time travelers either trying to prevent or ensure JFK's assassination being produced.

This thriving sub-genre was boosted with the 2011 publication of *11/22/63*, a novel by Stephen King. In the book, a teacher travels through a time portal to 1958 and attempts to stop Oswald from shooting Kennedy. Even before the novel's release, it was announced that it would be made into a film by Academy Award-winner Jonathan Demme.

The idea that Kennedy's assassination is a fixed point in time that cannot—or should not—be altered by time travel has been explored in several *Doctor Who* stories. The world's longest running science fiction television series, *Doctor Who* first aired on November 23, 1963. In TV

and book form, the show has made several ventures into the events of the preceding day. In his 1996 *Doctor Who* novel *Who Killed Kennedy*, author David Bishop shows that even a Time Lord cannot prevent the murder from happening, as the Doctor reluctantly helps a journalist and Kennedy conspiracy researcher travel back in time to become the killer himself.

As the passing years have provided distance, writers and filmmakers have become much more willing to indulge in playful depictions. BBC TV show *Red Dwarf* (1988–present) shows Kennedy assassinating himself, whilst adult cartoon *Family Guy* (1999–present) has shown Oswald killing Kennedy as a comic accident. Of course, another word for conspiracy is plot. Even if JFK were not historically important, a plot involving the murder of America's President by shadowy forces would be too good a story not to tell over and over.

FINGERS ON THE TRIGGER OF HISTORY

The distance of time has also changed the way the gunman who had his fingers on the trigger of history is depicted. Close to 1963, the actual assassin was rarely shown and named. In Alan Moore's seminal 1986 graphic novel *Watchmen*, it is only implied that CIA operative *The Comedian* is involved in JFK's assassination. By the 2009 film adaptation of *Watchmen*, the character is shown firing the fatal shot from the grassy knoll. A 1996 episode of the conspiracy-heavy show *The X-Files*, presented long-standing villain the Cigarette Smoking Man killing Kennedy in a way that gently mocks notions of conspiracy. In the same year, action film *The Rock* portrays the identity of Kennedy's killer as still having import, with Sean Connery's MI6 character imprisoned for decades owing to knowing the secret.

The Death of American Innocence—the Legacy of JFK

There is a persistence of grief that many millions in America and across the globe still feel for John F. Kennedy. No other leader's death—even those deaths caused by the violent cruelty of assassination—has ever induced quite the same sense of loss. Why? It is clearly not just about Kennedy as a man or President.

Many believe that grief for Kennedy is actually about him as an emblem of American innocence. There is a sense of loss for a stolen legacy that many feel he would have bequeathed if he had remained President and gone on to win the 1964 election, possibly handing the torch of hope on to Bobby in 1968.

Others find the continuing grief appallingly misplaced. Often these are the same people trying to debunk JFK conspiracies. They will suggest that his place in history is minor and any other president would have reacted to the forces of politics and economics in much the same way. Some actually attack conspiracy researchers for playing with a history that simply does not matter.

Should we treat the past as dead to us? Turn our faces to the future and move on from the death of John F. Kennedy? Poverty, injustice, war, and environmental degradation are with us in the present. Is it not better to turn our minds to understanding topics such as these rather than trying to figure out the answer to an old murder mystery?

History matters. It is the parent of the present. Beyond the reality-warping nostalgia and the glamor of the Camelot myth, Kennedy mattered. Certain individuals are gifted—for good or ill—to make a difference and set the course of history. JFK was such a person. That may be the exact reason why he was assassinated.

Had Kennedy lived is the big "what if" of modern history. There is solid evidence that among the likely "what if" actions are things that would have radically changed America and the world. JFK would probably have

tackled the power of the Federal Reserve. He almost certainly would have scrapped the space race and begun a mission to the moon with the Soviet Union. He would have made efforts to cool the Cold War. He would have pulled out of Vietnam and massively cut U.S. defense spending. These actions are the potential legacy of Kennedy that we never got to see.

Kennedy himself was no innocent. Here was a President who knew his 1960 election victory had been achieved with Mafia help. A bed-hopping President who slept with a Mafia boss's mistress. A President who smoked marijuana and experimented with other drugs. Behind closed doors, Kennedy was no reflection of his public image and no reflection of any of the innocence of white-picket-fence Americana.

However, the innocence America once possessed certainly died after 1963. It was not Kennedy's assassination alone that destroyed it, but rather his killing created a chain of unhappy consequences. Kennedy's death sealed the certainty of the Vietnam War and it was this conflict that ultimately cost America much of the innocence it had once enjoyed.

ABOVE Stolen Hope, Eternal Pride. A mule-drawn wagon carrying the casket of Dr. Martin Luther King Jr. is followed by dignitaries and thousand of people as it heads towards his memorial service.

LEFT "The Whole Bay of Pigs Thing." Were connections to JFK's assassination a factor in Nixon's actions over Watergate that eventually forced him to resign as president?

THE CONSPIRACY'S OTHER VICTIMS

If there was a conspiracy to murder JFK, he and his family were not the only victims. Beyond the blow to America and the country it might have been if Kennedy had remained President, the biggest victims of November 22, 1963 were Lee Harvey Oswald and his family. His mother. His wife. His two daughters who grew up without knowing their father. In a barely marked, barely regarded grave lies someone who lost his life as a result of the conspiracy and whose reputation was destroyed at the same time. Lee Harvey Oswald, the Marine who could not shoot fast or straight, placed in the official record as the lone gunman who stole the life of JFK. In the final analysis, what lies cold in the grave alongside Oswald is always the first victim of any conspiracy—the truth.

If Kennedy had lived, two certain and fully provable conspiracies—the killings of RFK and Martin Luther King Jr.—are unlikely to have come to pass. Together, the unholy trinity of these assassinations wounded the American psyche more grievously than JFK's individual murder. It was not just the execution of a single President, but also the destruction of a generation of inspirational leadership.

The final nail in the coffin for American innocence and the American people trusting their government came with Watergate. Many U.S. citizens believe there was a conspiracy involving their own government to assassinate JFK, but all Americans know President Nixon abused his power and lied to them.

However, many researchers believe the unfolding of Watergate is intrinsically linked to the events of Dealey Plaza. E. Howard Hunt, who organized the Watergate break-in, and the Cuban burglars who committed it are tied beyond doubt to the players in any conspiracy to kill JFK. Just before 18 minutes of crucial White House tape recordings were wiped, Nixon called the Warren Commission the "greatest hoax" and stated that the burglary opened up the "whole Bay of Pigs thing"—his phrase for the assassination. Did the bullets fired on November 22, 1963, ultimately end two presidencies?

We continue to live in the temporal shadow of Dallas. Great American comedian Bill Hicks made JFK's assassination and the cover-up of inconvenient evidence suggesting a conspiracy the focus of many of his most powerful routines. He articulated not just a sense of America's stolen innocence but also the stealing of the hope Kennedy represented. However many years passed, he was going to stay angry and keep demanding the truth. The shots that rang out in Dealey Plaza were still echoing for Bill Hicks. They still echo for millions of others too.

TOP Burried Truth. The simple grave of Lee Harvey Oswald at the Shannon Rose Hill Memorial Park in Fort Worth, Texas.

ABOVE There is a Light That Never Goes Out. An eternal flame burns at the gravesite of President John F. Kennedy at Arlington National Cemetery in Arlington, Virginia. His slain brother Bobby is also interred at Arlington. The bullets of conspiracy have failed to silence the inspiring message of hope both murdered Kennedy brothers give to Americans across the generations.

Index